STUDENT'S HANDBOOK OF SOCIAL ANTHROPOLOGY

Published by

Gyan Publishing House
5, Ansari Road
Daryaganj, New Delhi-110002
Phone: 011-47034999, 9811692060
E-mail: books@gyanbooks.com

Distribution Network
gyanbooks.com
India, USA, Canada, UK, Australia

ISBN: 978-93-7414-100-7 (PB)

First Published, 1936

2nd Impression 2025

Printed at: Gyan Press, Delhi.

STUDENT'S HANDBOOK OF SOCIAL ANTHROPOLOGY
Author: BIJAY CHANDRA MAJUMDAR

Owing to the antiquity and rarity of this book, certain pages are regrettably absent, and readability is compromised due to the blurring of the original text. If you possess any insights regarding the availability of these missing sections, kindly inform us. Your assistance is crucial in ensuring the completion of this significant work for the benefit of future generations.

STUDENT'S HANDBOOK OF SOCIAL ANTHROPOLOGY

BIJAY CHANDRA MAJUMDAR

GYAN

STUDENT'S HANDBOOK OF SOCIAL ANTHROPOLOGY

STUDENT'S HANDBOOK OF SOCIAL ANTHROPOLOGY

BY

B. C. MAZUMDAR

AUTHOR OF *Orissa in the Making, The History of the Bengali Language, The Aborigines of the Highlands of Central India, etc.*

PUBLISHED BY THE

UNIVERSITY OF CALCUTTA

1936

PREFACE

Nothing interests a man so much as Man. Even when this goodly frame, the Earth, appears a sterile promontory, man does not cease to be looked upon as the beauty of the world, a paragon of animals. How then Anthropology which helps to know ourselves, which traces the origin of Man, records the progress of Man and suggests on the basis of real facts the eternal possibilities of Man, has not been as attractive to the students as other sciences have been, is the question and this question has recently been discussed by some leading Anthropologists. The other day Prof. Karl Pearson raised this question in his presidential address at Cardiff in the Anthropological Section of the British Association in his usual forceful language.

Prof. Pearson in putting forward the high claims of Anthropology has said that though this branch of science should be the Queen of Sciences and should be the crowning study of the curriculum, it has failed to receive full recognition of its claims either from the universities or from the state because its utility has not been made clear to the state and the students have not been given to see that it opens a doorway to a career of usefulness.

The claims of Anthropology have not been taken seriously into consideration by the political and social reformers who need its aid most, as in their zeal to effect quick progress they are apt to ignore the truth which Biology has been clearly demonstrating that the very laws which operate in the material world, do operate in life without any deviation whatsoever. It has to be appreciated that it is impossible for us to control and guide the human activities merely by desiring to do so, by formulating a noisy scheme and by setting up an uproar without having recourse to the quiet methods of nature which Anthropology has been endeavouring to ascertain by studying the progressive processes of Life registered in all the works and institutions of Man.

Proud of his non-theoretical methods the philanthropist as a political agitator or as a social reformer speaks glibly in attractive eloquence of the slave mentality of men or of the pernicious superstitions of society (perhaps half muttering—O, cursed spite!) to set the disjointed things right, but does not care to learn how those phenomenal ills grew and does not care to learn from the very history of their growth the right natural method to be followed for their extinction or modification by having recourse to the form of labour which in the language of Matthew Arnold, in lasting fruit outgrows far noisier schemes and is accomplished in repose.

Know thyself, said Socrates to the inquirer who to be happy in life wanted to get a panacea for all sorts of ills which beset the human existence. This is exactly what the science of Biology, on the bedrock of which Anthropology stands, is asking all people to know. Come unto me all, ye heavy-laden, utters Biology to all, to teach what life is and to teach how to succeed in the unavoidable struggle for life. Biology tells us in no uncertain sound that we are not such stuff as dreams are made of, but are such stuff as the elements constituting the germplasm are made of—the germplasm which forms unmistakably the basis for all classes of living beings. We have to leave aside the subtle metaphysical question regarding the relation which subsists between mind and body, but have to learn, looking to the ever-increasing physical capacity of the bodily system, how the mind has been expanding more and more with ever-increasing activities and knowledge. To be happy as long as we may live by making the society in which we live happy, we have to learn this highly useful lesson and it is Anthropology which promises to teach this lesson.

To know aright then the nature and character of our physical, mental and moral activities and to be in a position to know what possibilities are in stock for us for our future progress we should know *first* how Man as a species has evolved with some special capacities and *secondly* under what conditions Man has been expanding his mind and sphere of action since the day of his arrival on the globe.

This handbook for students could not be intended to present all facts required to be discussed in Anthropology ; as an elementary work the following pages only aim at arousing the curiosity and interest of the students in this highly useful subject.

The useful science of Anthropology is a child of the 19th century; the progress, however, it has achieved by now is monumental. The late Sir Asutosh Mookerjee, whose illustrious deeds in the building up of the Calcutta University are bound to illumine the pages of its history for ages, introduced the subject in the Post-Graduate studies of the University when no other Indian University thought of doing anything in that direction. Now in the course of a few years the subject has been popular not only in the Post-Graduate Department, but also in the B.A. and B. Sc. Examinations of the University. This favourable reception of the subject encourages the University to introduce it in an elementary form for the students reading for the Intermediate Examination in Science as well as in Arts.

I cannot speak too highly of the value of some definite suggestions of Dr. Panchanan Mitra, Professor of Anthropology in the Calcutta University, which have all been incorporated to make this work useful as a text-book. I have also to acknowledge gratefully that Mr. Priya Ranjan Sen, Lecturer in the Department of English in the Calcutta University, very generously read the press proof of the following pages from start to finish with considerable care.

B. C. MAZUMDAR

CONTENTS

THE STUDENT'S HANDBOOK OF SOCIAL ANTHROPOLOGY

CHAPTER I

MAN AND HIS EQUIPMENTS FOR PROGRESS

Section I—The Spontaneity in Social Evolution

Specific unity of Man

The Science of Biology teaches us that man is a highly developed species in the animal kingdom and that for his immediate ancestor we have to recognise a high-class ape-like animal who may be called the proto-man or the tentative man. This biological proposition leads us to the history of the descent of man with which we are not directly concerned in this work. It is not the *descent* of man but the *ascent* of man with which we are specially concerned; by the term "the ascent of man we mean the continued progressive evolution of man in society since the day of his arrival upon earth. How long ago man as a distinct species came into existence, has not been quite accurately determined; but it may be said on a moderate estimate that it could not be less than five hundred thousand years ago. Man has been mentioned here as a species; what this signifies should be briefly stated to help us in determining many questions relating to the evolution of human society.

We come across, and are familiar with, various groups of man in various geographical areas who differ from us in physical appearance in some particulars. Even our children on meeting them do unhesitatingly and unmistakably recognise them as men, without forgetting to notice generally that they are different in physical appearance. Now, if any female of any of the groups be mated with any man of any other group of different physical type, the pair will be blessed with children and the children thus begotten will prove fertile when mated similarly with others. This fact of true breeding proves that men all over the world constitute one and the same human species. The history of the social progress of man, as we have proposed to narrate, will thus be the sociological history of all mankind.

Society a necessity

Men live in society everywhere on this globe. We can at once say, it could not be otherwise. A man, when born, is born a helpless child requiring parental care for many years. Again, it has to be noted, when this child is a child no more, but is a young man capable of earning his own living without requiring much help from others, feels strongly inclined under normal conditions to live with other men for his friends, companions and so forth. This strong desire on the part of man as we are familiar with, may appear to be an ordinary natural desire arising out of habits of life acquired during infancy. This cannot be denied, but there is another factor underlying this phenomenon, which the science of biology has disclosed to us and which it is necessary to emphasise.

Biology, or the science of life, teaches us that the desire spoken of above has its roots in the very germplasm which forms the basis of the life of all organisms of living beings from the lowest amœba to the highest animal, man.

Consciousness of kind

The biological proposition is: Any being of any particular species, whether low or high in the scale of life, knows the other beings of its species and becomes attached to them as beings of its own kind, as beings with whom it is inclined to remain associated. Every species is a fish out of water if not in the company of society of its own kind. Some facts of life are adduced here in support of this proposition of biology regarding consciousness of kind, as a clear notion of it is very much needed to solve many problems connected with the social and mental evolution of man.

Consciousness of kind in butterflies

One striking incident in the life of a butterfly, noted by Grant Allen in a story-book of his, is narrated here briefly to illustrate the truth of the proposition. A solitary egg of a butterfly of the orange-tip kind, gone away for good after laying the egg, is hatched on a leaf ; the little animal that comes out is a creeping worm in form, not at all the replica of a butterfly. This greedy green grub gorges for some time on the tender leaves of the plant and then sleeps as it were within the fold of some leaves. Then after a while it comes out of the nest of leaves as a full-fledged butterfly of the orange-tip kind, spreading the wings to sail on to an unknown destination. This newly born male orange-tip butterfly which never knew its parents, never saw any butterfly of its kind and never saw its own appearance in any glass, when on wings, meets butterflies of various other kinds flying about ; when, however, this male butterfly comes near a female butterfly of the orange-tip species, it recognises in a second the new being as its predestined mate, the one kind created for it, and commences to circle and flicker together in the full ardour of courtship. This is marvellous. The butterfly is, be it noted, a well-developed animal possessing brain.

Unicellular organisms

A species of animal of unicellular structure, very low in the scale of evolution, may be referred to for an investigation about this sort of instinct. This animal, as its structure indicates, does not possess the brain or any other organ and is only a small lump of jelly-like substance. For want of brain it does not possess the consciousness of self, but possesses, as a living organism, *sensitivity* and *irritability*. It absorbs what is food for it for its growth by its whole body and multiplies its kind (without taking another mate for the purpose), by being divided into two halves or by throwing off a portion of its own body; all the portions of the body thus divided become so many fresh independent animals without any need for establishing co-operation among themselves. It is yet a fact that when swimming or drifting about in their own colony they avoid (unconsciously of course) a locality in the water where there are unfriendly animals but do not avoid any inanimate object they may happen to come in contact with. Thus they show by their habits that they know an inanimate object as distinguished from the animate and they know their own kind as distinguished from another unfriendly kind. In this act of *knowing* they *do not know what they know* for want of brain, but show that they know their own kind and can differentiate other kinds by the contractions of their body, by their sensitivity or irritability, which is an unavoidable expression of life. Though these animals are not in need of co-operation with one another, it is quite curious that if one individual of this species is taken out from its place to another quite favourable locality in the water, the transported individual cannot thrive ; if it be carried to a spot where almost similar animals live, the transported animal contracts its body to signify its disapproval of the situation. If it be transported back to the colony of its own species, it shows by its movements that it has got back to its congenial home, though it has no capacity to know that its organism, by merely possessing what is called life and not possessing brain and consciousness, acts in response to the action of external stimuli and discloses the fact that to possess life even in its elementary form means (1) the capacity to know the animate from the inanimate, (2) the capacity to know one's own kind, and (3) the capacity to build up a society without being instructed.

The society of birds

Another illustrative example seems very much called for to strengthen the realisation of the truth that to come into and organise a society is an instinctive act flowing naturally out of the phenomenon of *life* itself. The example adduced is of birds who are no doubt required to pair together to form families and are required to live in pairs and to nurture the young ones as long as they have not learnt to live independently. Thus the pairs only are required to form a family with their helpless young ones, but are not required to live together in a society with other pairs of birds. Yet we notice a flight of birds constituted of several groups of families returning at sundown to roost together upon a tree, though each individual of the flight of birds gathered food for itself individually during the daytime, almost straying away from one another. Different families of birds do not co-operate with one another and yet they live and move together; this is no doubt forming a society due to an instinct imbedded in life. We find almost similar grouping together of many other animals in their natural condition (*i.e.*, when their natural grouping together is not disturbed or interfered with by man by domesticating them or keeping them at a great distance to secure man's safety), even though the families of the animals or the animals individually do not stand in need, like man, of mutual co-operation to withstand the attack of other groups, to secure food for sustenance, etc.

Samāja *versus* Samaja

Thus, according to the scientific conception of the term society, all living organisms, high or low, must be admitted to be living or trying to live in society. We may merely note here that failing to recognise this phenomenon of nature our Aryan ancestors in India drew a sharp line of demarcation between the aggregation of men and the aggregation of animals other than men; it is admitted, however, for some reasons a line of demarcation has to be drawn. They gave the term *Samāja* to the aggregation of mankind and the term *Samaja* to the aggregation of other animals to signify that animals other than men live together, merely because they are *born together*, as the term *sama* plus *ja* signifies. We proceed with this clear notion that life, which is a mystery to us, evolved and has been evolving by virtue of its innate qualities and tendencies all sorts of social institutions of man with slight differences here and there, because of differing conditions, careful notice of which will be taken in subsequent chapters.

Section II—The Nature of Life itself

It has been stated in Section I how society in its elementary form was bound to evolve by the natural, spontaneous urge for life itself which we share in common with all living beings or organisms of our world, but how the human society has expanded and is capable of being expanded by some conscious purposeful acts of human beings remains to be narrated. However, as in speaking of the purposeful acts of man the spontaneous activities of life should not be lost sight of, it is indispensable for us to know to a certain extent, though in meagre outline, the character and functions of life itself. Before attempting, therefore, to present a systematic description and explanation of human society as a whole, some aspects of life itself are set out below.

Definition of Life

We have spoken of the sensitivity and irritability existing even in the lowest possible living organism; we consider now some other essential characteristics of life. The science of biology asks us to hold life, or rather each and every living organism, to be an individuated entity capable of, by virtue of its constituent elements, automatically developing, preserving and reproducing itself. For these peculiarities some have called the living organism a machine ; true it is to some extent, an animal body works like a machine, but it is *self*-stoking, *self*-preservative, *self*-adjusting, *self*-repairing, *self*-multiplying and consequently it is much more than an ordinary machine. It should also be added exactly in the words of Sir Arthur Thomson, the eminent biologist: 'In the highest reaches of life *it is a self-conscious machine* which is a contradiction in terms.' This biologist has very nicely expressed the idea by saying that 'the organisms are more than mechanisms; life is a dance of enchanted particles with mind as the music.' The definition which Herbert Spencer has given of life is highly important and should always be borne in mind to consider the society-building activities in man. It is this: 'Life is effective response to surroundings.' There will be occasion to explain the full import of this definition but it is notable that accepting this definition as correct the biologist, Thomson, has added the memorable words: Life is the urge for more.

The urge for more

This exceedingly happy expression, *the urge for more*, carries such an idea as is bound to stimulate our thoughts in our inquiry regarding the secrets of life, even though it is being experienced that the central secret of life seems to retreat as science advances. It is very necessary to direct our attention to this innate tendency in the living organisms called the urge for more, since our progress in all directions depends upon it ; to live means to remain active and to struggle on without remaining satisfied with the present condition of things. To seek absolute rest by forsaking constant struggle tantamounts to one's becoming an inanimate object ; for a life to become inanimate is a contradiction in terms. True it is that every life or every organism is destined to die, but so long as it lives it strives to grow from more to more. To live means to evolve, and life means, therefore, the possibility of evolving. To attempt to explain fully this situation is to make an attempt to explain the whole of the idea of evolution, but that is not the subject which can be, or should be, discussed here. It should only be pointed out that activities or struggle of life, be they of man or other animals, bring about changes in the organisms and these changes are inherited by subsequent generations to work out the purpose (if that term be admissible) of the urge for more. Only a few points relating to this urge are noted here. A child moves its limbs restlessly and tries joyfully to stand up, to walk and to run about, disregarding failures, without knowing the purpose of the activities; but these activities do successfully help the child to grow from more to more. A grown-up man in his curiosity to know what is not within the ken of his knowledge, exercises his mental powers without being aware of the fact that by his struggle to know more he brings about such a change or such a convolution in the brain as is sure to expand the knowing capacity of the mind. The less this urge is in life, the less the growth of mental powers which are instrumental in evolving our society. It has been observed that some tribes such as the Bantus or the Bushmen of Africa, who do not live in big societies and live almost isolated in such a manner as not to get opportunities to exercise their mind very much, bring about a sad condition of the brain; even though they are in the prime of life there happens an early closing of the cranial sutures by virtue of which there is considerable loss in the power of thinking. In the civilised centres where minds of men are active, the cranial sutures are not so closed even in old age. We know of many eminent men of Europe who have produced original works of very high value even after attaining the 80th year. In ancient time in India it was believed by the Aryans that the power of clear thinking commenced to degenerate on a man's attaining the age of seventy-seven years seven months and seven nights when what was called *bhīmarathī* was believed to become the condition of the man. It must have been noticed by many that, in comparatively unadvanced societies in our country, men age very quickly and those who look very old untimely, exhibit senility very ordinarily. It is this urge for more which gives a healthy tone of freshness to life and its activities. We shall have presently to speak of various adventures of man to strengthen and develop the social organisation; it is this urge for more which stimulates the spirit of adventure. What the biologists have noted in this connection is a singularly marvellous fact that though there is a tendency in life to secure ease and peaceful security, the life impelled by the urge for more *does not necessarily follow the line of least resistance.* It is because of this *urge* that man can lay down his life quite joyfully when harnessed to execute work by surmounting difficulties.

Another fact is pointed out along with it. It has been said before that it is an inborn condition of life that it is self-preserving; it has also been noted that owing to the phenomenon of the urge for more, life disregarding knowingly or unknowingly the sure destiny of death goes on striving for a limitless more and more. These innate inner workings have developed in man such a strong love of life that he longs for eternity though he knows perfectly well that death is the sure destiny which awaits him. How this longing of man for eternity has led him to formulate many theories of life and to develop religious institutions in various forms in society, will be discussed in its proper place, but this fact as now here noted, should be borne in mind to solve various questions of society as will be delineated later on.

Section III—The Aptitudes of Man

In the two preceding sections notice has been taken of those qualities and natural tendencies of life which man in the main shares with other animals and which are very potent in goading man on to pursue the labours of society-building. We have now to take notice of those special faculties and capacities which man as differentiated wholly from other animals has been endowed with, and by virtue of which the human society has assumed a highly developed novel form.

True it is, man has inherited some habits of life from his ancestor, but the new qualities he has acquired through evolution into a wholly differentiated species, are what concern us here. Standing erect by poising the head on his shoulders and so forth, how the whole aspect and outlook of man's life have considerably changed, creating a great gap between him and the manlike apes, is very markedly exhibited, first in man's possessing an intelligent articulated speech and secondly in his mental power to 'look before and after,' to look forward with hopes and aspirations, to form the idea of an impalpable eternity, causing something like an indefinite feeling of indeterminacy in the matter of his existence.

"Man principally differs from the apes which of all animals he certainly resembles most by the truly biped mode of progress. Instead of holding himself in a bending attitude and walking supported on his arms, man walks erect. In harmony with this attitude his vertebral column presents three curves, cervical, dorsal and lumbar. This is faintly marked in the anthropoids and absent in the monkey and the curvature is more marked in civilised men than among savages. This is one of the conditions of the development of the brain as it assures the free use of hand and extended ranges of vision." (Denikker.)

How man's mind has expanded and is being expanded because of his awakened thoughts relating to the limitlessness around and about and beyond him, will be noticed in discussing the religious institutions of human society. As to man's intelligent articulate language a few points are only noted to arouse the curiosity of the students.

Human Speech

It is the frog which in the evolutionary scale of animals first produced the audible vocal sound. The frog in joy of life croaks loud and this croaking is not a speech; when seized as a prey by a snake it croaks in a different way merely indicating by the sound that it has fallen into danger. The case of the mimicking bird will appear different. A parrot reproduces the words it learns, but this it does by merely memorising those words without learning the meaning thereof. That portion of the brain which helps to memorise words is well developed in the mimicking birds and is definitely connected by nerves with the vocal organs, but the nerves of the vocal organs in these birds are not connected with that portion of the brain which has been marked out as the seat of intelligence to a certain extent. The mimicking birds do not, and certainly cannot, hold conversation among themselves. It has been observed and recorded by some expert men of medicine that when the intelligence-area of the brain of a human patient is impaired, the patient ceases to learn the meaning of new words; the patient can only reproduce from memory what he previously committed to memory exactly like a parrot, but does not exhibit the capacity to attach any meaning to the words uttered.

A dog which perhaps has been the earliest companion of man as a domesticated animal, makes various sounds to express various feelings; the following words for various vocal sounds of a dog may be referred to, which only indefinitely signify what sort of impelling feelings are at the root of the sounds. The words are: baying, barking, growling, howling, moaning, snarling, whining and yelling; beyond uttering such sounds the dogs do not converse either with men or other dogs. How very different our intelligent articulate language is, capable of being changed and improved, need not be explained by illustrations. There may be many expressive gestures of many animals and many sounds caused by many feelings, but human speech and intelligent gestures are widely different not only in degree but in kind.

We all know pretty well how the advancement of civilisation has been due to the human faculty of speech and consequently there is no need for detailed discussion here. It has, however, to be always borne in mind in considering how growth has been possible for human societies by communicating with other societies.

Men communicate with each other by gestures and words, by various signals or by writing. The American Indians of Dakota had an elaborate gesture language. By signals which could be seen or heard primitive peoples used to spread important news. By lighted fires the tidings of a beast killed, etc., were made known in South America. In the Canary Islands whistle language was much in use. Among the Bantu Negroes of Africa there was a highly developed drum language.

Other capacities of man

Now we proceed to take note of some other powers or capacities of human beings which though continuing to be very helpful, were once exceedingly helpful to the primitive man in organising and developing society. We at times raise questions as to how it was possible for primitive men to live in safety and to thrive well with their undeveloped intelligence; but if we look to the physical capacities of the primitive man in ancient times as detailed below, many of these questions may be partly answered.

About smelling: Higher power in this matter is easily observable in many lower animals. The bees have been rightly declared in biology to be living in the world of smell, looking to the fact that those tiny animals with very tiny brain and tiny organs of smell move to distant places to get the honey they seek. Similarly we notice how the very tiny creatures, the ants, get scent of the sugar kept by men far away and climbing up high get to the spot where sugar is. This shows that the power of smelling as in man does not depend necessarily upon high brain powers. It was widely reported in 1934 that a black man of lower culture in the company of some white men at a place in Australia did not allow his white masters to camp on a spot of ground as he smelt the existence of a poisonous serpent underneath; in their curiosity the white men turned up the firm soil at the spot in question, following the directions of the black man, and found actually a poisonous snake there. How the primitive men could, because of this power, select a safe site for their residence and how they could be aware of the approach of unfriendly beasts, can very easily be imagined. The power of a dog in this matter is too widely known to be described in any detail. This animal is known to have been the earliest companion of man. That a dog can recognise one man from another by the smell of the body, is very well known.

It has been hinted at in the very opening paragraph of this chapter that by migrating to different geographical areas the various races of men have come into existence by developing different physical types. For various reasons (some of which will be noticed subsequently) these races of men are generally averse to mix with one another ; that because of the smell of the body one race is disliked by another, is a thing of interest. Tylor who is regarded as the Father of Anthropology, writes: "It would be possible to tell a negro from a white man even in the dark by the peculiar satiny feel of his skin and *the yet more peculiar smell* which no one who has noticed it, is ever likely to mistake." This instance will give us the clue as to how, when in conflict, men of one race could be distinguished from those of another in primitive times, even when features of the contending races were not very markedly different.

The Andamanese can discover certain fruits in the forests a long way off being directed by the sense of smell.

About hearing: It is known to many that the people of the wild and the semi-wild tribes in India detect the movement of men and beasts from a good distance by pressing one ear upon the earth. The word '*krośa*,' literally a loud cry, is the term for the distance of two miles and a half in India, at which distance the loud voice of a man might be heard. It will be narrated shortly how the primitive people requiring extensive lands for each family had to live very much apart, though forming one compact clan. This fact of the power of hearing of those days explains to some extent how living apart the people could assemble together at a moment's notice.

About seeing: It is a fact that people of lower culture are known all over the world to possess strong eyesight. Tennyson speaks of our blinded eyesight as the result of our pouring over idle books.

The acuteness of the sense of sight is greater amongst the primitives and the percentage of people with acuter vision is more amongst the dark-haired than the fair-haired.

We have considered in this chapter how man has been equipped with various capacities to be fit for the struggle of life and to be evolved differently from other animals on the globe.

CHAPTER II

The Adventures of Man

Section I—Fishing in addition to Fruit-gathering

The evolutionary processes in effecting unceasing continued changes in living organisms and in transmutation of one species into another, have been all throughout so exceedingly slow and imperceptible that no new species coming into existence could perceive, even where perception as a mental act could be possible, that it became, at its origin, a newly differentiated something, fresh from the hands of nature. The human beings at their birth as wholly differentiated from the proto-man could not be aware of their advent on the earth as a new startling fact of significance. Every individual was born as a child, of father and mother, being taken care of during infancy, inheriting the instincts and habits of life of the ancestral stock. What should constitute his food and how to earn his food were not problems with him to start with and he did follow the usual known and accustomed course of life. The *family* was already there as will be particularly noticed in a subsequent chapter, no matter how marriage was then performed.

Were not hunting and fishing for meat and fish diet in addition to vegetarian diet pursued by the proto-man ? We cannot say yes or no, though we are very much inclined to answer in the affirmative. It will not be very correct, we fear, to decide this question by merely observing what the apes generally eat who are arboreal in habits, while proto-man greatly removed from the apes, was, as has been rightly suggested by some biologists, terrestrial in habit and character. "Man's ape-like ancestors were mainly vegetarian, living upon fruits, nuts, young shoots and the like. Before man became a hunter he was a food-gatherer he got what he could in the way of plant food and probably added to it such insects, grubs, reptiles, birds and mammals as he could lay hands upon." (Harrison.)

It can never be ascertained with confidence that what is called fishy smell proved nauseating to those who are principally frugivorous or vegeterian in diet. In taking stock of facts in this direction it may be quite safely said that only a small number of tribes (perhaps for special local reasons) disdains fish but the majority of the savage tribes are found very fond of alternating their diet with fish. There is no such aboriginal tribe in India as is not fish- and meat-eating. We know that some civilised people in Europe have now acquired the taste for a few sorts of fish quite raw. It has been observed among the savages in different countries that even those who get fruits and vegetable food in profusion, do procure fish and meat to make their meals specially enjoyable. The savages, who do not usually eat fish or meat, do resort to hunting and fishing at times of drought; so it could not but have been with the early savages too. This fact has been accepted as correct by all anthropologists.

It is a great fact that in old times when swarms of men were moving on to various quarters of the globe in quest of food, and when permanently settling down with agricultural occupations was not possible, the people who took to fishing could form colonies of some permanent nature more easily than others following other occupations could From the salmon-catching Red Indians of British Columbia to the fishermen of Orissa inhabiting the upper reaches of the Mahanadi, there are many of the fishing occupation who may be cited in support of this proposition. Fishing was not so difficult as it appears to-day, looking at the fishing net and other devices of comparatively advanced days. It is found almost everywhere in India that to catch fish the people set up a hedge-like barrier across small streams and spread mats over the hedges ; the fishes moving on in the streams leap up on getting to the barrier of the hedge and fall on the mat cleverly spread over the hedge to fall a prey to the fishermen. The device of making a fishing cage of bamboo sticks as all are familiar with in India was not very difficult to hit upon and perhaps the fishing rod could also be devised at an early time. In the rocky parts of the Mahanadi the fishermen very cleverly spread some small branches and twigs of trees in the rocky niches in the river bed to catch with great ease a good number of lobsters ; because of the low character of their intelligence, the lobsters do not avoid the traps and are always deceived. Fish of the eel class can easily be caught in bamboo tubes in the mud in a river or in a tank. Another device for catching fish is now mentioned which depends upon the use of fire by man. It will, however, be shown presently that man's acquaintance with fire was not so late as is generally supposed, though it might be that he did not employ it to cook his food for some time. The device spoken of is this. During night time, specially in dark nights, the fishermen of Orissa light some bundles of faggots (locally called *hoola*) and carry the lighted bundles along the edge of the river. Various sorts of fish in their light-tropism come close to the edge of the water in shoals and the fishermen dip their peculiarly made baskets in the water to catch them.

The various modes of fishing in vogue in various parts of the world are as follows :

(1) *By the hand*, as by the Australians and Papuans ; (2) *by the sagai* as by the Australians; (3) *by the harpoon*, as by the Ainus ; (4) *by shooting with bows and arrows*, as by the Andamanese ; (5) *by the gorge*, with a long arm and bent end ; (6) *by fish-hooks*, straight or curved, with barb or of several pieces ; (7) *by means of flying kites* with nets attached, as in Indonesia or Melanesia ; (8) *by various snares and traps and nets* ; (9) *by barrages* in streams ; (10) *by animals* such as the cormorant or otter or dogs, as by the Chinese or Ainus ; (11) *by poisoning of water*, as by the Kharias of Chota Nagpur, etc.

Fishermen in old times got a very profitable occupation to live a happy life. We get it in history that the fishermen on the banks of the Ganges became once very well-to-do people and by living in comfort evolved very attractive physical appearance. It is in the historical record that Riṣi Parāśara and Rājā Sāntanu, both ranking high in the Aryan society, married maidens of the fishing class. "While hunting peoples never formed civilised states, fishing population became at times trading communities like the ancient Phœnicians." (Harrison.)

Use of Fire

Now, before proceeding to speak of the hunting occupation a word seems necessary on the early use of fire by man. It is admitted on all hands that forest fire is very common even to-day in the forest of India and it is only by issuing strict rules that the British Government is trying to keep it down. Man as a specially intelligent being cannot be considered to have been indifferent to this occurrence when he commenced roving about in quest of food. He could observe how the beasts in the forest ran away terrified giving men the opportunity of killing some of them and some of them perished in the conflagration, and getting some half-perished animals for food. To discover fire or to light a fire by a device is one thing, and to be acquainted with the use of fire is quite another. It cannot perhaps be said that men in those early days could not, with perfect safety to themselves, collect some burning wood, or to keep alive the fire could not put some dry sticks on it, either to warm themselves or to keep away unfriendly beasts. Men in those days of dim past might have been following the accustomed ways of eating either raw or sundried fish, but of their not taking to the method of roasting fish or flesh in a rude manner on the hot ashes nothing can be assured.

Fire was made by primitive man (1) by friction which included (*a*) ploughing as by the Tasmanians, Australians and Assam tribes; (*b*) sawing a tree trunk by one or two sticks as in Australia or Burma; or a stick by a creeper as amongst Nagas, or bamboo splits by bamboo splits as by the Paniyans of Malabar; (*c*) rotation by hand-drill, strap-drill or bow-drill or pump-drill, the first being more universal as in ancient or primitive India; (2) by percussion as by flint against stone or metal against stone; (3) by compression of air or fire-piston as in East Burma and Malaysia; (4) by mirrors and lenses as in modern Sikkim.

Along with what has been said it has to be borne in mind that such has always been the character of the human brain that at the striving of man, impelled by the urge of life for more, there occurs a response in the brain to the surrounding conditions to develop better intelligence. This is partly why Herbert Spencer defines life as effective response to surroundings. How men in their migratory movements had to come upon and to live in some unfavourable regions, has been related in the first part of this work; now by referring to the progress of human beings despite many adverse conditions Dr. Lowie has remarked in his Introduction to *Cultural Anthropology*: "They excite our admiration that in unfavourable regions they turn to account such resources as nature allows them."

Section II—Hunting and other Occupations

It cannot be accurately set down in order of sequence as to which occupation the early man followed first and which next, but that hunting became a great occupation in early times is undoubted. Though not needed at present, the people all over the world exhibit a passion for hunting and are found to take delight in going out sporting. The aboriginal tribes of India give us expert *śikārīs* acquainted with the habits of life of the denizens of the forest. The naturalists in their work of scientific interest in the Himalayas requisition eagerly the help of the Lepchas of Sikkim who are not at all bold and adventurous but are very well informed of the details of life of the plants and animals of the mountainous regions. It is also notable that all aboriginal people keep dogs, though it is difficult to trace how the art of domesticating dogs, so useful in hunting and guarding houses, could be easily acquired by men all over the world from the earliest time.

The hungry generations of human beings required, no doubt through all time, flesh of animals for food, but hunting could not be the sole occupation of mankind at any part of the world, for all men from the earliest days were required to pay special attention to gather, throughout the year, all sorts of edible products of plants which formed, it seems, their principal diet.

Hunting has been done (1) by weapons, (2) by traps and snares, (3) by hawking and (4) by running down the game. The first two are used by primitive peoples. Hunting by weapons is the most primitive and universal. Originally the weapon was but a stick, or at a distance a stone. The earliest hunters of the Old Stone Age more than 100,000 years ago used hand-axes for hunting small game or sharpening wooden weapons for such hunt. The weapons of offence, generally classified as those used for stunning and crushing like clubs, those for piercing like spears and arrows and those for cutting like swords, were used either by the hand or affixed to a long handle, and most of them were as effective in hunt as in war. The throwing weapons which are (1) those thrown by the hand such as a club-stick, axe, knife, javelin, sagai, boomerang and harpoon and (2) those set free by a mechanism which includes the (*a*) projections by an artificial arm such as a spear-thrower or sling, (*b*) projection by a pressure of air, *e.g.*, the blow gun, were the same for the war and the chase. Besides these two artifices only used for hunting are the lasso or a sort of hand-noose thrown over the head of the prey in North America, and the Bolas (Spainish *Bola*, ball) or thongs with several balls for capture used in South America.

Hunting by traps and snares is very wide-spread. Snares, (1) with horizontally extended thread were used for catching quails and other birds in Egypt ; (2) with vertically extended thread were used for catching deer by Dayaks of Borneo, or gazelles by Africans and polar bear by Eskimos ; (3) with cylindrical threads are used in East Africa for catching rats. True traps are of six types : (1) those with glue for capture of insects or birds, (2) those with weight which is loosened shutting the door on the prey in the trap ; (3) those with strings and radiating points ; (4) those with spring in action working (*a*) by pressure as for catching elephants by Sakai of Sumara, (*b*) by a bow as for entrapping elephants in Malacca ; (5)

those with bent cords; and (6) those with firing devices.

It has been rightly suggested by anthropologists that women who have always been physically weaker became principally the gatherers of fruits and edible vegetables, while adult men, stronger in limbs and physically more fitted to run about, engaged themselves in hunting.

Earliest division of labour

There was thus established from earliest times a division of labour between men and women. The women because of their physical constitution are more fitted to execute the sort of work which demands dull patience and careful, deft handling. The women while collecting fruits and roots and other plant products had to keenly observe many facts associated with the growth and decay of the plants and so to start with they could not but become gardeners and farmers by their training. Again, as they were bound to become mothers, they could not but be given such tasks as have to be accomplished in a state of repose. To gather fruits from tall trees they were not required to climb up the trees (specially of excurrent growth), for the device of using poles for the purpose was very simple to hit upon. It has been observed that some apes by thrusting one bamboo into the hole of another can gather fruits from the top of such branches of trees which cannot be reached by climbing by the apes though arboreal in habit. It has also to be noted that it was easy to observe how the sideshoots of banana, for example, were removed or thrown out at a favourable spot and how many seeds or bulbs thrown out here and there could multiply the plants. The women, therefore, very naturally became the keepers of the houses and became horticulturists and crude agriculturists to supply food and comfort to all.

Hunters required home

When men had to be out hunting by organising a party, they had to travel some distance which they did not mind and were required to come back in due time to where their women-folk and infants were left. It was an uncertain game with them and they could never be certain of always getting animals for food or getting enough meat for the food of all. The occupation was a bit precarious and consequently to reserve a place where some vegetable food was sure to be obtained, was a necessity in addition to the necessity to get a safe place to take rest and sleep. By depending wholly upon a precarious living, requiring hard work, the hunting hordes could not afford to travel on and on with their wives and children, not knowing where they might get at least a shelter for their much-needed rest. Men no doubt migrated on and on in early days, but this they did not, and could not, do without settling down for some time at such a favourable place where food of some sort could be earned with certainty. It was never possible for the migrating hordes to leap into the unknown ; they must have made some permanent colonies somewhere and when they increased in number and required fresh field and pastures new, they advanced to form fresh colonies getting to know in their long excursions the favourable character of the place of their new colonies. To make colonies, and colonies of a permanent nature, became a matter of vital interest with these men, for without forming permanent settlements they could not run up gardens and could not become farmers to get a sure source for supply of daily food. The peoples of nomadic races always moving on from place to place could not but be required also to measure every inch of ground, for it was hazardous to all to come suddenly upon an unknown region.

Pure hunting peoples required large areas for their means of livelihood. A primitive group rarely exceeded 2,000 in number and each of its settlements generally contained one or two hundred persons. In Australia there were eighteen square miles for each person before modern colonisation whereas in highly agricultural areas elsewhere there are several hundreds to a square mile. In Chota Nagpur, a Kharia village contained only one or two families and in Assam there were settlements with only one or two huts.

Manliness called forth in hunting

The hunters no doubt must work much harder than the gardeners and tillers, but the male people who were hunters tasted in their hard pursuit for life the sweets of manly energy and fearlessness called forth by the task and so they grew in love with their task, and did not necessarily settle down to gardening and farming.

Intelligence and discipline

This occupation did not make them dunces, for they could and did improve their mental powers by always devising new methods to obtain success even when they did not invent nets and other traps and could not forge instruments of metals for killing animals. They had to study the habits of animals to lead them to fall into a pit covered with loose earth and leaves of trees. It is by studying carefully, and to a degree scientifically, the habits of animals that they could domesticate cattle for their use and employ horses to carry them with speed from one place to another. The writer of these pages knows personally that the wild savage Savaras of the Sambalpur tract entrap very successfully a good number of quails (called *baṭer* or *guruṇḍu*) by mimicking at a suitable time the vocal sounds of the quails by keeping themselves unseen at a hiding place. It can be said that all sorts of works, calling forth energy and skill in cooking, help men to develop their brain powers. It is to be specially noticed in this connection regarding the hunters of primitive times that they, developed among them that social discipline much needed for the organisation of society. To obey the leaders and strictly to co-operate with one another, could not but be the traits of the organisations of the hunting party.

Industry

Our chances of error in studying the hunting societies are not very much, for primitive conditions of hunting, fishing and gathering of fruits, roots and crude cultivation alongside the hunting occupation, lasted in full vigour at various parts of the world even a century ago. How by pursuing the fruit-gathering occupation some tribes devoted mainly to fishing could thrive well, has been observed in some Pacific islands where chickens and pigs were raised and Taro and bread-fruit trees were grown along with the cocoanut. The cocoanut tree alone proved highly valuable; the fruits for food, the leaves for baskets and mats, the wood for carving weapons from, the shells for cups and bowls, the oil for smearing the body with and the husk for fibres to make highly useful strong ropes, are familiar examples. It should also be mentioned that the occupation of agriculture could very well flourish without even knowing the use of the plough. The plough is used since olden times in the areas of Hindu, Chinese, Islamic and Western cultures. In primitive areas there was terraced cultivation, or turning of the soil by a hoe or use of a digging stick. It has been noticed and recorded that even at such a late date as the discovery of America by Columbus, the American agriculturists did not know the use of a plough, though they and the Oceanians had been successful farmers for centuries. It appears that the Savara-Kol people in the highlands of Central India used sticks for a long time for digging the soil and only at a comparatively late date

Uses of the plough

introduced the plough for agricultural pursuits.

Medicine

To give examples of the development of intelligence of the savage people, both men and women, mention may be made of their knowledge of the medicinal properties of some plants. Some medicinal drugs which are unknown in the pharmacopoeia of the Aryan physicians here in India are in use among the common people and are known by the name *ṭoṭkā* (coined from Sanskrit *truṭ*) medicine in Bengal. The nomadic Bediās did, till the other day, carry on surgical operations and many women of the aboriginal tribes of the Bhandara district in the Central Provinces do even now come to Bengal to sell various roots declared to be of potency to cure many diseases. It has been natural in these advanced days to set them down as quacks, but it will not be wise to consider them all as so many cheats. Often these primitive doctors or medicine-men combined magic with their practices and were very powerful in their society.

Trade

That the savage people of various tribes, though living wholly apart from one another, conducted in the remote past some trade among themselves, is a fact of great importance in studying the mind of primitive men. There was a good deal of "the silent trade." A stone implement was kept in the place where it was made and it disappeared and an animal skin was kept in its place. Periodic meetings between groups, exchange of luck-bringing fetishes or charms, semi-religious trading voyages of particular groups, ceremonial distribution of wealth, such as the Genna ceremonies of Assam or '*potlatch*' of American Indians were several methods of exchange of goods among primitive peoples. Dr. Lowie has justly remarked, by noticing some facts worth remembering, that international or intertribal trade is not a new development in modern civilisation ; he remarks that even paleolithic Belgian cave-dwellers used flint peculiar to districts of France whose residents surely exacted some compensation, and Babylonians got gold from Egypt, iron from the Hittites, cedars from Lebanon and so forth. These facts show that culture could diffuse in early times even without there being wholesale wanderings of peoples.

Savage races did not stagnate

About the continued progress of various races of men of lower culture we are apt to form wrong notions looking to the speedy development of scientific knowledge among the advanced people of to-day, but we must bear in mind that in bygone days the *savages multiplied themselves everywhere and did not stagnate.* This could not have been possible without continued expansion of mind as exhibited in social development. It was not generally the case that as a result of following the sort of occupations in life spoken of and hinted at above that the primitive societies stood still like Joshua's moon at Ajalon. It is true that owing to some circumstances of the modern age which cannot be legitimately described here, many societies have deteriorated and some have died out altogether, but the primitive societies, we shall see later on, are capable of expanding themselves to develop the growth of a higher civilisation in co-operation with the other progressive societies which, we should remember, have come to be what they are by being successors of some savage societies of old.

Art

Two instances bearing evidence of the high skill and of the sense of beauty of primitive men may fitly be mentioned here; it has been brought to notice that incised tools, ivory carvings and clever animal paintings date back to more than 40,000 years ago in the caves of France and Spain and possibly between 50,000 and 100,000 years ago craftsmen made their arts and crafts in graceful shape.

Position of women

One word is added to what has been said above of the early division of labour among men and women. It has been suggested that what fell legitimately to the women for their task they most naturally undertook to execute for the well-being of society. Never in the early history of the society of man were women thought to be of low rank for doing what was their part of the duty in life. Very permanent happy conjugal life is noticeable among various classes of people of lower culture. The women never resented their situation but on the contrary performed their task most joyfully. When the menfolk, to give an instance, give warm covering for the body of the people by supplying the skins and wool of many animals, the womenfolk supply the wearing apparel for constant use by beating the barks of trees thin ; we need hardly show that this use of the bark was the precursor of woven cloths, and perhaps for the weaving of later days the women were principally responsible. Now in modern times when the ancient hard work of the male people have been made easy of performance, when perhaps the courageous and dangerous work involved in conducting war is becoming so simplified that by merely pressing some keys of a machine all the work needed may be performed and when it is thought that the domestic duties hitherto entrusted to women may be performed well by some paid servants, many women have been resenting their situation by considering it undignified. Whatever may be the future of the old order of things regarding the division of labour among men and women according to their natural aptitudes, it should be remembered both by the conservatives and the progress-seekers that there is dignity in every labour and no class of work, if properly conducted, can stand in the way of man's mental expansion; it should also be remembered by looking to the natural aptitudes of both the sexes that men are liable to a heavy penalty if there is even an attempt to disobey laws imbedded in the life of human beings.

The character of early settlements

Various were the occupations of the early savages and in pursuing their occupation steadily they wanted to settle down at a fixed place to avoid constantly keeping anxious moments. Nothing has been said in these pages of the growth of pure nomadic habits among some of them ; that these people too could not do without carrying with them such articles as could be easily adjusted to afford shelter to them, can be confidently asserted. Those who settled down in villages in early times, were required, when pursuing principally the occupation of hunting, to live as much near one another as possible; but as agricultural, or rather the fruit-gathering, pursuits could never be disregarded, they required extensive lands for their villages and when this agricultural work increased speedily, the families forming the unit had to live much apart from one another; this living apart did not stand in the way of their assembling together at short notice for reasons mentioned in Section III, Chapter I.

How the villages multiplied with the increase of population is described in the following chapter; it is only pointed out here that in proportion as the agricultural and industrial occupations increased, the hunting excursions began to decline as a regular pursuit of life.

CHAPTER III

Expansion of Human Society

It will be seen presently that men, swarm after swarm, had to migrate to different regions of the world in quest of food and to set up their permanent habitation. The physical anthropologists have tried to show that by these migrations to different regions of different climatic conditions, and for some other reasons as well, they developed in themselves differently, some well-marked physical changes resulting in bringing about some varieties indicating different physical types; but it should be remembered that in developing their societies they had to follow, or rather were actuated to follow, those very laws to which all human beings are subject. They differ from one another in many habits of life but underlying these various habits there runs such a current regulating the activities of life as is common to all human varieties. Based upon this current or rather upon the essential and universal principle of life, evolving various social forms and types, a general biography of man as a united whole can be narrated and that is the scope of this handbook. Taking all humanity as a single unit we can roughly mark off some stages in the growth and expansion of society to give the culture history of mankind.

Multiplication of settlements

Each group, say, of close genetic affinity was divided and redivided to establish new settlements not always in close proximity to the original settlement. Names had to be given to all such settlements for their proper identification. How these settlements were given new names may be partly surmised from the names of many villages, with the meaning of which we are familiar. We can see how such a name as Bānsbeḍiā (surrounded by bamboos) in Bengal or Kolābirā (*kolā*—tiger and *bir*—forest) in the Sambalpur tract could come into existence. It was easy to give and thereby to know the names of villages, looking to their physical characteristics. To indicate that people of such and such groups were of such and such villages, the village names might not have been adopted by the people as their surnames, though in most cases this was so done but the people outside the groups always spoke of them by the adjectives formed of their village names. Again, the physical characteristics of the villages were bound to be changed in many cases and men of short memories did not, or could not, remember that because of some physical characters of their lands they were being called by the names of their villages or settlements. The settlements are thus the starting points of social and political life. Those related by blood and family ties try to remain together. In hunting tribes, there is a special hearth for each individual small family, may be in a cave marked by boundary stones as among the Veddahs of Ceylon. Some hunting nomads use caves for a temporary dwelling and some hunting-fishing tribes like the Andamanese have a wind-screen for the family and a community shelter for the whole group. The pastoral nomads have to remove with their cattle and sheep from winter to summer quarters every year. The crude agriculturists with the digging-stick and hoe also move and change their gardens and fields. It is only agriculturists proper who have permanent settlements. It is also a fact that the people of various villages of various names were required in course of time to live elsewhere, retaining all the same their village names as specially reminiscent of their old-time groups. The social and economic unit was formed by the kinship association of the clan or *gotra* named after some traditional ancestor or ancestral place personified. Thus when at a remote subsequent time the names of some animals, plants and so forth were found associated with their names they, with their comparatively unadvanced mind, could imagine they might have descended from the animate or inanimate objects joined with their names. The origin of man was always unknown and some mythical interpretation of an origin might be easily formulated in those early days. In the opinion of the writer of these pages this phenomenon seems principally responsible for the belief in totemic origin prevailing among peoples of lower culture ; many tribes all over the world do still believe their origin to have been from a hill or a plant or an animal.

Belief in totemic origin

Further, it may be noted that some persons showing unusual heroism are believed to have descended from, or to have been protected by, a lion or by such other animal ; many such stories are current in India regarding the origin of some noted families. The Aruntas of Australia, for instance, had totem groups representing all possible animals or plants found, one named after Kangaroo, another after a flower, a third after the Emu bird, a fourth after a grub, each, so to say, protecting the food or animal for the rest of the tribe. Marriage was regulated by classes and not by totem groups. What, however, stands out is that with some totemic or other sorts of names a large number of groups of men was known among all the groups (originally perhaps of kindred affinity) to belong to the same or to different clans. In the clan division some groups were regarded as of mother's clan and some of father's clan as will be seen later on to avoid close interbreeding. Amongst the Veddahs, for instance, where simple families of parents and children, their married daughters and sons-in-law lived simply in cave-shelters, each individual belonged to a *waruge* or clan reckoned through the mother and nobody could marry within the clan and the marriage of children of brothers and sisters who belonged to different clans was the rule.

Clan division

What has been said is of the simplest group division developing a simple sort of clan. How in the formation of new and newer groups many complex things happened, may now be illustrated with a few examples only. In the expansion of societies it was not possible for many societies to be constituted wholly of the descendants of one and the same groups of men, as assimilation with others in the course of migratory movements could not be avoided. In Assam the Kuki tribes tend to break into divisions of two (dual) or three (tripartite) groups for marriage purposes and these perform useful functions in the community but gradually when cut off from each other these form new clan groups.

New social contact

In the course of their expansion many people of one cultural tradition came very near to other settlements of other cultural traditions either to be united or to remain apart in spite of closeness of habitation because of some marked difference in culture. In India we still find many aboriginal tribes living in contiguous isolation; in the settlements, for example, of the Savara-Kol people and of the Kandhs, though living in close proximity to each other, the Savara-Kols speaking their own speech and maintaining their own social customs remain apart from the Kandhs of different speech and social habits and do not in any social matter mix with one another. These people of aboriginal tribes do not even drink a glass of water offered to them by their Hindu neighbours under whom they always work as labourers to earn their living. This sort of isolation has arrested the progress of the aboriginal tribes and they are miserably deteriorating, losing slowly their intellectual powers. Another fact relating to these aboriginal tribes is noticeable: it has been recorded by some eminent persons like Sir W. W. Hunter, that when some of them, by forsaking their social habits and by adopting a veneer of foreign culture, are separating themselves from their own people, are losing lamentably many good traits of theirs. This is perhaps an example of not following the natural evolutionary processes in life.

It is, again, very remarkable that the people of Aryan descent and proud of Aryan culture settling among the vast multitude of non-Aryan peoples in Peninsular India have forsaken their Aryan speech and have adopted the speech which is designated as Dravidian, though in social matters they remain widely apart from their non-Aryan neighbours.

Another very significant fact of social contact in India may now be noticed. A few people of some aboriginal tribes by losing their independent position at their partial or complete disintegration sought of their own accord the protection of the people of Aryan culture, now called Hindu, and obtained the protection and shelter they asked for. The Hindus could not consider those people, of a different sort of cultural tradition, fit to be welded into their own organisation ; the newcomers were, therefore, regarded as foreigners, dissimilar to them in all respects. These foreigners or newcomers were, however, given perfect liberty to live and manage their social affairs themselves either by following their own traditions or by adopting new methods if they would choose to do so. The Hindu society, constituted as it is with Brahminic supremacy remained all through wholly apart from the social organisation or organisations of the newcomers ; this credit should be given to the Hindus of old that they never interfered with the social rules or conduct of these remnants of other tribes.

In this connection a word may be said regarding the civil government of the Hindus. The Hindu society or the Aryan society of Brahminic supremacy was constituted of many communities, no matter whether they were related to one another bearing some genetic affinity or not. The king of this society, who could not but be the political head, was required, in all matters of civil disputes relating to the customary laws of the communities, to give judgment strictly following the rules and customs of each and every community and not by legislating new things for them. The rules of law which appear in many Dharmaśāstras were only ideal rules prescribed for the Brahmins and for some other high caste people, but were not codified laws as our European rulers, accustomed to codified laws, considered them to have been by mistake. The Rajas were required to adjudicate all matters in the manner aforesaid and this method was called ruling according to Dharma. The disputes of the newcomers of the disintegrated non-Aryan tribes were also decided exactly in the same manner. Thus in social and some civil matters all the communities in the Hindu society were in a manner loosely connected together but all the communities did not come together to constitute a nation in the sense the word is now used. Those who are called people of the depressed classes have become so by failing to work themselves up properly ; they have generally failed to be awakened with the consciousness which would make them utter: 'Man 's a man for a' that.'

Social amalgamation

Let us now turn our attention to cases of social expansion which resulted in bringing about unity among various hordes or tribes of different cultural traditions. One horde or tribe coming in conflict with another, in seeking expansion by acquisition of new lands, brought about changes of various nature. If the agression of one tribe could not be resisted by another, a compromise might be reached ; both the tribes, if they were not wholly dissimilar, might occupy by a sort of division of lands of one and the same geographical area, to be welded later on into one tribe or to be tolerated to maintain separate social situations almost on equal terms. In the latter case the two tribes became only two communities of one tribe. It is in evidence that when various groups of men were welded into one tribe, the newly formed tribe by swelling in number and by mixing new blood could become very powerful and progressive. Conflicts which intensified struggle of life called forth new energy and stimulated intellectual activities. It is an admitted fact that when society expands and new thoughts pour in because of the influence of the new elements in the expanded society, the growth of intelligence becomes rapid. It has, therefore, been rightly said that social milieu forms the growth of intelligence. Auguste Comte once remarked that men became more and more moral as the human society expands. In this connection it has always to be borne in mind that in early times there were incessant migrations, displacements and unions by mixing of blood ; and in the case of unions various racial types were blurred or blended into one, and thus new mixed types were formed.

Thus groups starting with the family and blood relationship in the clan came to form in many cases organised possessors of land and army units under a despotic ruler binding them into a sort of feudal system as amongst the Bagandas ; or the purposes of hunt requiring many units drew together many allied tribes as the Red Indians of North American plains ; or tribal councils are federated together into powerful tribal league for purposes of war as amongst the Iroquois of North-Eastern United States and Canada.

Struggle *versus* War

It is to be carefully noted that for a society to expand, the struggle of life should increase. This struggle in its normal form at the urge of life to get more and more does not mean killing off one another : it is indomitable energy and endurance with which an organism develops or evolves. It is however, true so far as facts recorded in history go to prove, that without there having been war consequent upon the national aim for a high objective, no people has hitherto achieved a situation of power commanding elements of progress.

Social contact and race prejudice

As to the influence of war upon society a fact has to be carefully mentioned. It has been previously shown that man moving out in quest of food inhabited different parts of the world and thereby developed different types of races and social institutions of various kinds. Now at the present time some of these races after attaining great progress are seeking new regions for further expansion. In this attempt they are coming upon many races of the world which so long remained in comparative isolation. By remaining in isolation, the peoples throughout the world have, in course of their own racial evolution, formed strong race prejudices and consequently contact with one another is being strongly disliked. It has been noticed before how the smell of the body of the Negroes is strongly disliked by the Europeans. That the physical features and the colour of skin of one race are abhorred by another, is also a widely known fact. They all hate one another and yet they have been forced in a manner to come close to one another.

Race prejudice

It has been stated as a biological truth that man knows his kind and is naturally attracted to the individuals of his kind; along with this we have to consider how in course of their evolution various races of men come to hate one another by developing very strong race prejudices. Surely the only means by which these prejudices may be overcome is to come close to one another, but in this coming together conflicts are sure to arise to produce disastrous results. It is expected, however, that in course of this inevitable conflict all races will in their inborn self-preserving tendency or instinct learn that, howsoever high or low, all races of the world have something to contribute to the development of a larger world-wide society. The science of biology has been teaching us that the building up of such a large world-wide society is the "great far-off event" (we could say, 'divine event' also in the language of Tennyson) to which whole social activities have been moving.

The eminent biologist Thomson, following another and equally eminent biologist, Sir

Arthur Keith, after duly considering the fact that those young tribes that had no prejudices in favour of keeping themselves to themselves would tend to disappear, says the following memorable words: "We must ask ourselves how far it may now be necessary to correct our inborn race prejudices by a sense of the interdependence of the peoples of the world and their interests. We may surely learn to care more for other peoples without lessening our love for our own country."

Definition of Some Terms of Social Forms

Family (পরিবার).—In Anthropology this term indicates 'a group consisting of a man, his wife (or wives) and their dependents, children, own or adopted,' *e.g.*, an Andamanese family or a European family.

The Extended (or Joint) Family or Gross-familie.—'A group of families related genealogically (বংশীয় বা বংশানুক্রমিক) (or by adoption) and living together as a well-defined family,' *e.g.*, a Hindu joint family under a *Kartā* generally the seniormost male member in authority.

Patrilocal—when the family lives at the father's place.

Matrilocal—when the family lives at the mother's place.

Clan (*cf*. গোত্র).—A group of persons reckoning their descent from some common ancestor *unilaterally* (*i.e.*, on one side exclusively) and marrying outside the group to which they thus belong. When the child takes the band of the father, it is a *gens* and when he takes that of the mother it is a *clan* (according to American Anthropologists) but *clan* is generally used for both types. The word *sib* is also used in this sense, meaning a group which generally marries outside the group and a *Father-sib* (পিতৃকুলগোত্র) and a *Mother-sib* (মাতৃকুল-গোত্র) are terms used at times to indicate the groups reckoning descent from the father and mother respectively.

Sept.—A subdivision of a clan or used synonymously as a clan (*cf.* গোত্র and প্রবর)

Phratry.—Two or more divisions of a tribe containing a group of clans which generally marry from another group of clans within the tribe. Thus many Kuki tribes have two such divisions called *dual organisation*, or they may have three and be called *tripartite*. Thus if *kulin* and *maulik*, or *kulin* and *srotriya*, groups could marry only in the other group, they would be either *phratry* or *moiety*.

Kin and kinship (জ্ঞাতি, আত্মীয়).—Relationship through common descent or by adoption.

Affines and affinity (কুটুম্ব).—Relationship through marriage.

Tribe (জাতি).—A group of a simple kind, designed by a specific name possessing unity in speech or dialect peculiar to the group, claiming possession of a definite range or habitat and constituting an interbreeding or intermarrying group, *cf.* Kuki, Naga, Santal, Bhil, Gond, Toda, Veddah, Andamanese, etc.

Caste (বর্ণ, বা জাত).—Social groups which marry within themselves only, as in India or amongst the Maoris; *e.g.*, Brahmin, Sudra, Subarnavanik, Kumhar, Dom, Nair, etc. (India). Each of these consists generally of several clans marrying outside their own clan.

Descent (বংশানুক্রম)—determines the relationship to a clan or such a group by birth. It may be *matrilineal* (মাতৃকুলানুক্রমিক), *e.g.*, amongst Khasis or Nairs, or *patrilineal* (পিতৃকুলানুক্রমিক) as amongst ourselves, Europeans, etc.

Inheritance (উত্তরাধিকার)—determines the heirship to property; thus, amongst the patrilineal Hindus the sons, amongst the patrilineal Europeans often the eldest son alone, amongst the matrilineal Khasis the youngest daughter, amongst the matrilineal Nairs all the daughters, inherit the property.

Succession (পদাভিষেক)—determines the holding of an office in the family or bigger groups, *e.g.*, succession amongst the patrilineal Hindus to the office of the *kartā* is generally by the eldest male member whatever his share in the property; amongst the Nairs succession to a similar office is by the seniormost maternal uncle, or amongst the matrilineal Garos by the youngest son-in-law.

CHAPTER IV

The Marriage of Man

Man inherited, as has already been said, the social habit of living in family from his ancestor, the proto-man. This necessarily implies that marriage as a system must have existed in the society of the ancestral stock, no matter in what form the couple was joined in marriage and no matter how long the united couple lived together as husband and wife. It was, however, believed by some and is still held true by some that men and women, to begin with, lived in a state of promiscuity or married in groups without caring to be united as so many couples to live together either permanently or semi-permanently. This wrong notion was due in the first instance to the unscientific idea that for a system to come into existence a sort of disorderliness must be postulated previous to the orderliness of the thing, in false analogy, say, of our

Promiscuity—a wrong idea

building a house by collecting materials: A chaos in the beginning is an unthinkable thought in science. In the second place wrong interpretation of some primitive customs led the early writers to form the notion in question.

The history

We proceed now to take stock of such facts as are calculated to give us the true history of the marriage of man. By marriage in human society we mean a regulated conjugal relation, sanctioned and recognised by the society, between men and women. Now we have to ascertain if this regulated union has been the result of a measure of expediency adopted by men or it has been due to the natural tendency in this direction imbedded in life itself. To do so, the habit of pairing together among lower animals has to be observed with care.

In taking note of the habit of lower animals in the matter of sexual union we exclude such animals as are not required by nature to take care of their offspring, for mating for the purpose of organising family life to take care of the offspring, is not of any interest or value to them. The birds forming pairs are required, we know, to take care of their young ones for some time and so we look to the habits of birds in this matter which have been very thoroughly studied by many naturalists among whom the name of Dr. Brehm is very notable. Dr. Brehm has recorded, and his record has been found correct by others on careful examination, that most birds excepting a few species (as, for example, the fowls we are very familiar with) when pairing do so once for all till either one or the other dies. Dr. Brehm has said in admiration for the exemplary family life of the birds that 'real genuine marriage can only be found among birds.' But marriage is really social recognition of a biological union and is better restricted to human society. If the simplest need of propagating the species and of preserving the species was only concerned in the matter, the birds might dissolve the union when the need for rearing up of the offspring would cease, but they do not do so. It is very important to note

Union of birds

in this connection that only when the female bird feels impelled to become a mother the feeling of its male companion is awakened to perform the biological function of propagating the species and not at other times. Yet the two companions (not required to co-operate in obtaining food) do not part company; they live together merely for the sake of living together and express their joy of life by going on singing by keeping up close companionship. Referring to this fact the biologist Thomson says: "Man may learn from the birds not to stop singing when the honeymoon is over."

Value of courtship

It is highly important to remember this significant fact to discuss the question of promiscuity among men, that it has not been the habit with the male birds to leave it to chance to meet a female when required for companionship (which they could do far more easily than man) but to form durable attachment for the selected female birds they court to evoke very tender feelings. We, again, refer to Sir Arthur Thomson on this point and quote his words: "Very characteristic of the bird-mind is the strong current of feeling, whether it be in the patience of brooding or in the ecstasy of courtship."

Domesticated animals

It is universally admitted that the animals which have been domesticated by man have lost their real natural habits by coming under the control of man; they cannot select partners as they could in their independent living in the wild natural state. As far as it could be ascertained, most quadrupeds are distinctly known to live in pairs and do not go on changing the male or the female companion. It is very difficult to recognise one beast from another by well marked signs when they live wild in a forest, yet it has been ascertained to some extent that the pairs continue to live as constant companions even when it is not the pairing season.

It will be very relevant to consider the habits of apes who, though far removed from men, are the highest among lower animals in the scale of evolution and closely resemble men in physical type. Naturalists affirm that the chimpanzee, like the gorilla, lives in a family and builds nests for the young and the female on a forked branch, and that the male himself spends the night lower down in the tree. He is, writes Westermarck, induced to do so by an instinct which has been acquired through the process of natural selection because it has a tendency to preserve the next generation and thereby the species.

Now that we observe that animals reaching higher and higher stages by the process of evolution have acquired the habit of living in pairs and of living in family, it cannot but be admitted that man who has been the highest in the scale of evolution must be admitted to have been living in family and this habit of life of his could not but have been a primeval one inherited from the ancestral stock. It is monstrous and horrid to think that men and women ever left it to chance to meet together to multiply the species. The physical necessity of men and women of proper age to live constantly together is very great and it is horrid

Promiscuity could not be possible

to think that to meet the demands of this necessity men and women were at any time callously ready to accommodate one another, and natural likes and dislikes counted for nothing. The tender feelings, on the development of which depends the development of humanity, cannot develop if a durable attachment between men and women be not formed, and the children born in the family be not taken special care of. Not by chance satisfaction of physical thirst, can a man or woman be blessed with that emotion to unfold the high qualities of mind, which the enduring conjugal affection can confer upon him or her. It is a noted fact in the character of men and women that when they get children and naturally develop affection for the children in rearing them up, this affection or attachment for the children reflects upon the parents to increase the conjugal affection.

The children who are protected and nurtured by their parents develop a sort of feeling for the parents which is a mixture of reverence and affection and this feeling of reverence and affection is wholly incompatible with the sexual sentiment. The children, while living with their sisters and brothers, play and quarrel with one another and thus develop among themselves a sort of familiarity which does not, under normal conditions, allow the sexual sentiment to grow among themselves, for the new feeling born at and after puberty tends to grow in the environment of newness. When the new feeling grows after attaining puberty, which is in character incompatible with the feelings for parents and brothers and sisters, a new emotion occurs in the mind which it is not possible to display before the parents and brothers and sisters. This feeling flares up when a stranger appears in sight to one's liking. To a young man a young girl appears as a new lovable object, differing altogether from objects too familiar to arouse a new emotion; she is a "phantom of delight" when she first gleams upon the sight.

The root of Exogamy

Without discussing the whole philosophy of love it may be pointed out that the wife of a son brought into a Hindu household has to keep her face covered and is not allowed to speak to the son in the presence of others. No matter whether this custom was brought into use to keep love alive, it is a fact that this keeps up the freshness and newness of the wife to the son of the household. To seek the bride, therefore, from outside the family became very naturally the usage in society.

When a usage of natural growth is maintained in the society for some time, it settles into a custom specially in the primitive societies and is never allowed to be violated. Men and women thus acquire in course of time a strong aversion against marriage with the members of the family or the families closely related and much acquainted with. Such a feeling of aversion, or a prejudice if some would like to call it so, has a great survival value in the domain of biology for it has been ascertained that sexual union with those who are closely connected in blood leads to degeneration. This rule is followed among some lower animals merely at the instigation of the life instinct, *e.g.*, it has been observed in an animal of such a low order as the bee. The naturalists have carefully noted that bees of one and the same hive do not meet together in sexual union ; the bees of one hive are mated with those of another hive when they move out in pursuit of their duty of collecting honey.

It is true that young men seeking girls for their partners in life sought the hands of girls of other families, but these outside families could not but be known families, for connection with altogether unknown individuals could not be liked either by the marrying parties or by their parents and friends. Consequently the unions were in the beginning among known related groups and so the unions were then endogamous, though close breeding might be avoided in the unions. Generally speaking, as shown in the previous chapter, each and every village contained groups of men closely related to one another in blood. When villages were divided or split up into many units or rather, strictly speaking, when with the population going up new colonies or new villages were established, men generally of genetic affinity peopled all the villages of the neighbourhood; and for that reason the union in marriage of the individuals of different villages did not amount in early time to pure exogamy. When, however, in course of time the people of different villages came to be known by their village names or totem names and were considered to be men of different origins in different villages, the people, in accordance with their growing tendency to form marriage alliances with those who were not closely related in blood, developed among them the custom of marrying off one male of one village with a female of another village. Without detailing all the intermediate stages it may simply be said that some villages which were remembered to have originated by the overflow population of a particular village, were considered by the people of that village as the villages of paternal clan, and those villages from which brides were obtained for some time were marked off as belonging to the mother's clan. To start with, therefore, the people of one and the same tribe were divided into father's clan and mother's clan, though they all bore genetic affinity to one another. It was then established as a custom that brides should invariably be chosen from the girls belonging to the mother's clan, bearing certain totem names and recognised by those totem names. By the way, the author is inclined to believe what some Erengā-Kols say, that for their once supplying long ago *erā* (wife) and so necessarily *engā* (mother) to the Muṇḍā-Kols, the Muṇḍās (who do not intermarry now with the Erengās) gave them the name Erengā.

Marital union not connected with religion

In all probability, the celebration of marriage was in the beginning unaccompanied by religious rites. There are many primitive tribes or tribes of low culture among whom, we know, religious rites do not form any part of the celebration of marriage; the Savara-Kol people, for instance, invite their own people to come and eat together at the wedding and make it a festive occasion for dancing and singing together. What they do is to notify the new union to all members of the community, giving the fullest chance for the community to know that the marriage has been performed correctly according to the custom of the community; their eating and dancing together signify their approval of the union.

As to starting a new life by the married couple, a word should be added. Where the father of the bride required, say, for want of adult male labourers in the house, the services of the bridegroom, the bridegroom might be required to live in the house of the father-in-law; otherwise the bridegroom would under ordinary conditions take the bride to his paternal house. It may, however, be said, considering what takes place in the majority of cases in India among the primitive tribes, that the bridegrooms set up independent living by starting new households for them.

Post-nuptial living

The general moral effect of setting up independent households by the married couples is not very small. Though the members of the paternal houses and other near relations rendered helpful co-operation, the newly married

Monogamy favoured

couples had to work independently for themselves arousing in them the feelings of the importance of individuality and personal responsibility. Again, as the wife in the house was not, as a regular rule, allowed to visit her parents in their house and as her husband, except on some festive occasions, had to be present in the house for daily work, a married couple had to form a deep attachment for one another excluding the chance of forming any attachment with other persons. Other individuals, both male and female, of the neighbourhood or of the village, could seldom get time during the working hours of the day or even during night time to visit other houses merely to chat on some pleasant or unpleasant topics. Sensuous or sentimental talks with others could not very much influence the minds of the married people in early times. These circumstances were helpful in the beginning developing a strong sentiment for monogamy. We find as a rule in the primitive societies in India that they all adhere to the rule of monogamy, though there is no declaration of principle in that matter. The Kol people of the male sex in the Chota Nagpur area having now been greatly influenced by the social rules of the Hindus, are known in some rare instances to indulge in polygamy.

Polygamy

It is hardly possible to point out one or two causes to explain the origin of any social institution ; all the same, a few facts which seem responsible for polygamy may be mentioned. When many persons in the primitive societies became very well-to-do and could afford to give food and comfort to many, their marrying more than one wife could become possible. It has been said that the wives in their newly set-up households could not get (perhaps did not also require for want of leisure) companions to talk to, to get relief in their humdrum sort of life. Now, when the father of a bride-elect could see that the son-in-law intended was very well-to-do and his daughter was not to return to his house and might be feeling too dull to live alone in the house of the husband who would be busy with many things, he might easily propose to give away some sisters of the elected bride in marriage to the elected son-in-law. Perhaps the system of marrying many sisters together, which is called *sororate*, came first thus into use. Many rulers and zemindars of the Oriya-speaking country send some *pailis* or young maidservants with their daughters to the houses of their sons-in-law, explicitly for the purpose of keeping their daughters company. Another example of a fact known to the author is also recorded here. A Gond woman in the Central Provinces would be delighted with a second wife for her husband to be relieved of her multifarious duties in the house. It need not be mentioned here that these people cannot afford to keep paid servants.

Loss of dignity of women

This fact is of great social significance that the women commence to lose their position of dignity in the house and begin to be treated like slaves when polygamy prevails in society. We can see, therefore, that the womenfolk, at least in the polygamous societies, do not at all favour this system of marriage. In some rich families where male successors become a need because of some religious ideas, marrying more than one wife is felt as a great need to get a son to succeed to the father's property. In Europe where monogamy has been strictly established Napoleon Bonaparte was forced to take a second wife to leave a son of his blood to succeed to his empire.

Polyandry

The system of marriage called polyandry, *i.e.*, one woman taking many husbands, is so very rare that we can at once say that the system could not take root at any part of the world. The system exists in Tibet; in India, it exists among the Nairs and Todas of the south. When several brothers marry the same woman it is *fraternal polyandry* as amongst the Todas. When the husbands are not so related, as amongst the Nairs, it is *non-fraternal polyandry*. In Tibet it has been noticed that because of this system many brothers with one wife can be kept permanently together to earn a living which is difficult for the unaided efforts of individuals.

Regarding the origin of the system at a corner in South India nothing definite has been known. It has been thought to have been due to the scarcity of women in certain cases, specially where infanticide prevailed; or it has been the result of a desire to keep the family property intact as among the Todas.

Hypergamy

One word regarding what is called hypergamy. Men of some culture in a society did not lose much on the side of culture if they married eligible women of some families or communities of a lower culture, for the women seldom getting chance of meeting their own people could very easily be raised to a state of higher culture by the husbands. If the women, however, were allowed to be married by persons of lower culture, their undesirable degradation could not but be very much feared. That with this idea girls are given in marriage to men of higher status or dignity is in evidence in all societies.

The facts stated above serve to show that the general tendency of life to grow in comfort is to favour monogamy in marriage; and it will bear repetition to say that absence of monogamy in marriage has very much lowered, and tends to lower, the proper situation and dignity of women.

Some Customs defined and illustrated

Patrilocal marriage.—Marriage is called patrilocal when the wife lives with the husband, *e.g.*, as amongst the Hindus, Europeans, etc.

Matrilocal marriage.—Marriage is called matrilocal when the husband lives with the group of his wife, *e.g.*, in the case of घरजामाई amongst patrilineal Hindus, or in most cases amongst matrilineal Nairs, Garos, etc.

Prohibitions of Marriage

There are generally certain laws prohibiting marriage in certain cases.

(1) *Incest*—is 'sexual intercourse between prohibited degrees of kindred,' *e.g.*,

amongst all generations of father's relatives or three generations of mother's relatives among the Hindus.

(2) *Exogamy*—is 'the prohibition of marriage of any individual belonging to the same social or local group,' *e.g.*, ভিন্নগোত্র marriage among the Hindus where nobody can marry in his own গোত্র.

(3) *Endogamy.*—'Rule prohibiting a person from marrying outside a certain social group of which he or she is a member,' *e.g.*, a Hindu has always to marry within his caste. Thus castes are endogamous while *gotras* are exogamous.

Injunctions or Preferences in Marriage

Levirate—so-called from the case of Levi in the Bible—when the younger brother married the elder brother's widow, *e.g.*, as among Vedic Hindus or still among some Hindus.

Sororate—when a man marries his wife's sister. This is considered as good form by the Hindus, while till recently it was considered illegal in England to marry a deceased wife's sister.

Ortho-cousin marriages—are between the children of two brothers in patrilineal descent or between the children of two sisters when it is matrilineal. Where exogamy prevails this is prohibited as ortho-cousins will always belong to the same clan. Among the Arabs and Muhammadans this is allowed.

Cross-cousin marriages—are between the descendants of a brother and a sister. It may be of two kinds as when a man marries his mother's brother's daughter; this is very common among the Hindus of South India; or when a man marries the daughter of his father's brother. Both types may occur together.

Modes of Marriage

Marriages may take place by

(1) *Elopement* (পৈশাচ বা রাক্ষস) when a bride is forcefully carried off. In a more violent form it was *marriage by capture.*

(2) Mutual choice (গান্ধর্ব) when the husband and the wife select each other.

(3) Exchange (পাল্টাঘর) " when two men exchange sisters as wives or daughters as wives for themselves, their sons or brothers."

(4) Payment of dowry (কন্যাভরণ) or bridegroom price (বরপণ). This is generally the প্রাজাপত্য marriage of the Hindus. Similar forms, earlier practised, were ব্রাহ্ম and দৈব.

(5) Payment of bride-price (কন্যাপণ) as in some cases among the Hindus and was called আসুর. In many primitive tribes, sometimes as among the Kukis one may serve for certain years in the prospective father-in-law's house in lieu of payment of bride-price.

CHAPTER V

RELIGION

Very strong sentiments which men evince in most societies all the world over in adhering to their religious faiths of diverse character prove incontestably what high value men put upon the institution of religion by being vitally interested in the upkeep of that institution. As this highly prized institution is wholly peculiar to human beings, its origin as well as its various notable forms must be carefully noted by adverting to the nature and tendencies of the human mind.

Man as an animal agrees with other animals in many matters relating to the functions of life, but differs entirely from other animals in his mental capacity not only to think but to think with reason, to form a judgment not only by taking account of his past experience but by contemplating a likely future that awaits him and in forming a notion of something eternal which surrounds him and is beyond himself. How because of the evolutionary changes effected in the body in his physical make-up he can think of an impalpable limitlessness about him, can think of an eternity outside himself and can with conscious hopes and aspirations brood over the thoughts of a future, is like all origins shrouded in mystery.

That animals other than man cannot think of eternity has been admitted by the scientists. It will no doubt appear quite clear that the animals including the apes can think of the detached particulars of the objects they come in contact with while engaged in securing food, in avoiding danger and in other similar acts, but cannot think, like man, in terms of universals. An intelligent animal knows itself and others and sees the birth of animals but does not or rather cannot think like a man to ask in its mind how life originates; it goes on doing things as a daily routine, following the inherited and acquired instincts, but never busies itself to consider that in its dealing with others of its species how it should behave or what should be its right or wrong conduct. It sees death occur and may at the death of one of its species be frightened temporarily but neither does it think of the dead for a very long time, nor brood over the destiny that awaits it. Again, in the urge of life for more the animals do many things to secure food and other necessary things by engaging at fight at times, but in this very urge man attempts to accomplish 'what is next to impossible' as Goethe puts it. How in his contemplation and exercise of mind in the manner indicated above, man has changed the character of his society and has created a new outlook for himself can be studied best by investigating into his activities in organising religious systems.

In this investigation we will meet with such human thoughts as may be declared now to have been once illogically spun out, but if we bear in mind that at the basis of them there is the new urge of life for more, born of man's new mental capacity to contemplate on human destiny, then it will be admitted that there is much method in his madness or illogical thinking. We proceed to give examples.

The soul or the double of a man

Man does not like to die though he experiences that death occurs daily. How in primitive times man, according to his wishes, could come to the belief of a soul that survives death, has been beautifully explained by Tylor and Spencer. The view is briefly stated here.

Men when retiring into their caves at night put always such barriers in front of the caves as could not be removed even by strong animals; when asleep in these caves they as a matter of course dreamt many dreams, but when at a place away from the caves the dreams were remembered as a consistent whole relating to active actions by them, they could not but very much wonder, for they did not consider the dreams to be unreal. For instance, they had the dream of a hunting excursion involving many successful and unsuccessful pursuits of theirs. When awake in the morning they found the caves as well secured as they were at nightfall; how could then they get out at night by removing the barriers to hunt, as they had dreamed? It was a puzzle to them. Other experiences of the primitive men must be joined to this thought to see how the problem was solved. The thought that the images of theirs as they could see reflected in water, and the shadows of theirs that ran quickly with them through thickets and stone barriers, could not but be their doubles; they were considered to be real, undying souls, imperishable in fire and water, and these doubles, they thought, forsook their bodies, while they were asleep, to accomplish their feats of hunting which had formed the subject of their dreams.

A statement like this of the anthropologists may be considered by some as merely imaginary, but we can see that these primitive notions are noticeable among people of far higher culture. Clear corroborative evidence of the existence of this sort of notion and of man's assigning high value to dreams can easily be gathered from the common people in all countries, for in the first place people of all grades of culture do still survive almost in all parts of the globe, retaining their primitive notions and faiths, and in the second place there has not been in the advanced societies such a thing as the wholesale uplift of all individuals to higher cultural notions.

We have said how the primitive men came to the notion of an undying soul. How this notion grew stronger and some new social habits were formed, will now be stated. When a man working hard in the sun fell into a swoon it was supposed that the real man or the soul walked out of the body of that fatigued person and so his friends, to induce his soul to come back to the body, sprinkled water on it to make it again a fit abode, muttering their request to the soul for its return. When the man in deep swoon or in a state of trance did come to his senses, it was believed that the departed soul returned in consequence of what was done for the purpose. Then, again, when a man actually died, the people expecting the soul to return bathed the dead body with water and offered it food. When, moreover, the person who died, happened to be an important leader of the society, the people continued to do many things to get information of the departed soul, as is still done in some islands of Melanesia. In their thoughts for the departed soul, some saw him and had some conversation with him in dreams. This experience led the people to form a device to meet the soul of the leader at times of need to get his counsel. Timid people were not ready to create artificial dreams for the purpose, but some courageous fellows offered their services and did actually bring about a state of trance by fasting and by adopting other means to be in communication with the departed soul.

Fasting

As to fasting as a preparatory measure it may be said that by fasting one could get suitable physical weakness to fall into a state of half-consciousness. There was also another idea connected with it ; the disembodied soul, it was thought, was averse to come in contact with a person in whose body cavity there might be many impure things like the stool ; to become pure the wizards purged themselves of the impure things, and did not eat any food which originated impure things in the body cavity. These medicine-men

The priests

or mediums, or priests, who were always small in number, were held in respect even by the king himself for they revealed the much needed advice or direction given to them by the departed souls or ghosts. Again, to obtain pure and fit persons for wizards, the class of the wizards was kept aloof, unmixed with the common people, and was given to procure sons by marrying girls of their own pure class ; when there was any failure in the ordinary manner to get a suitable wizard, one from among the common people was taken into the wizard class by some purificatory ceremonies.

Another fact in connection with the death of a mighty leader or of a king should now be noticed. It was believed, as will partly be seen in considering the origin of the magical rites, that the primitive men believed that by absorbing a bit of the body of a mighty dead man many qualities of the dead hero could be possessed by a man. Following this notion some people at some places did actually eat the flesh of some persons in a ceremonious fashion. It has been pretty well ascertained now that men who knew their kind could never be inclined to become regular cannibals, but it was only by following some religious notions that men occasionally ate the human flesh. There are some mystical *tāntric* rites in our country for attaining superhuman powers which recommend partaking of human flesh and some *yogīs* are known to have done so on rare occasions. To eat and drink symbolically the flesh and blood of the dead sacred hero or demigod, is still now in vogue in some civilised societies to obtain religious merit.

Eating of human flesh

What is specially to be noted in this history is that notions and acts narrated above are not connected in any way with the conception of man generated by his natural perception of the eternal not-ourselves. True

Notion of soul unconnected with notion of God

it is that this natural perception of the impalpable eternity has been instrumental in giving man his idea of a Supreme Divinity from which everything proceeds including the ghosts and other objects worshipped by the primitive man ; but the primitive man in very early times did not refer to the Supreme Divinity or, for the matter of that, to any divinity at all ; on the other hand, he was fully conscious that it was definitely a ghost or the soul of a departed man that he worshipped and sought to appease.

Sacredness of the dead body

In holding the departed souls worthy of worship the savages held the dead bodies to be more sacred than the living bodies of men and treated the dead bodies with great veneration. This notion of the savages regarding the dead bodies is largely shared by almost all civilised people to-day, though the ideas of the savages regarding the relation that may subsist between the departed souls and living men, have considerably changed. This shows that the old notions unconsciously survive through succeeding times.

Growth of patriotism

It has also to be remarked that savages by keeping themselves in touch with the departed souls developed very strong patriotic sentiments for the geographical area they inhabited. They thought that the souls of their ancestors or of their people lived unseen in their lands only and so their own country became an object of great love. Malinowski has noted that in some islands of Melanesia the people think they are always in direct communication with the dead souls of their people ; in the howling of the wind these savage islanders can hear that some dead souls are wailing in the wind seeking opportunity to be reborn in the wombs of some females of their society.

Magic and fetish

Very closely connected with the worship of the souls of the ancestors is the system of invoking the powers of inanimate nature to come to the aid of man. Without discussing what the character of the conception of the primitive men regarding inanimate nature was, which they knew no doubt as inanimate in sharp contrast with living animals, we should better cite some examples to show how in some cases the inanimate objects were treated or dealt with by them. It seems rather clear that when the primitive men utilised their needed materials to build huts or kill or frighten unfriendly animals, their thoughts were not directed toi nquire of the occult virtues of the materials and they only used them without thinking of them much as we all do now. Though they could notice the plants to grow and to die they treated the vegetable kingdom as inanimate like the inanimate running water or the non-moving stones. When, however, the savages used some plants or their products for medicinal purposes they contemplated their special potency with special attention ; while eating, however, the plants and their products, they did not pay any special attention to their potency as they had been accustomed to eat them from infancy. In using, for example, the juice of the leaves of some plants the savage people came upon the idea that the plants (which they practically treated as inanimate) could infuse their inner virtues in men. This idea led them to believe that stones if properly selected (by some wizards, of course, noted for their knowledge of inner mysteries of things) could infuse in men their strength and durability of life when worn on the person ; some other stones or metals, therefore, came into use as amulets for acquiring strength and keep away some dangers of life. This belief in the efficiency of the amulets is even now world-wide and the European peasants of many countries do still wear amulets, getting them from some persons believed to have knowledge of their mysterious power. In this idea we only notice the belief in the natural virtues of things and do not notice anything distinctly of supernatural character.

Amulets

How, however, a conscious spirit was believed to be residing in inanimate objects, can be illustrated by the rain-making art or magic of the savages which is still practised by the people of lower culture in many parts of the world. When it rains, the clouds

The spirits of things—rain-making

like smoke in appearance gather in the sky, roaring sounds are heard from above and flashes of lightning resembling fire are seen. At times of drought it was thought that the conscious spirit of rain could be induced to cause rain, if things similar to clouds and lightning could be made to appear, for it was believed that the rain liked to come down at the sight of those objects. The people then lighted a good fire to cause clouds of smoke through which the flashes of light could be observed from above as flashes of lightning, and to cause a roaring sound the people either rolled down pebbles from a hillock near by or beat drums to produce roaring sound. If by some chance rain then actually poured down, the people on needed occasions repeated this experiment. Generally speaking the rain-makers became successful, because they practised this art as magic at such times of the season when following a drought it was usual for rain to come down. The rain-makers were pretty sure of the success of their magical performance, but yet in their anxiety they murmured some words in the form of prayer in persuasive language to soften the heart of the spirit of the rains. Why the people could believe in the efficacy of the prayer (which should rather be called an incantation) should be explained. It was a matter of common experience with all that if supplication be made in a suitable language showing humility, the hearts of men could be softened down ; exactly in analogy of this the *mantras* or prayers or incantations were composed and used. It should also be noticed why the *mantras* composed at a past time continued to be in use in all succeeding times.

Incantation

On occasions of failure to bring down rain, the rain-makers did not lose faith in their cult (as often observed among people in all matters of their faith), but thought that all particulars of the magical procedure were not correctly observed or perhaps those *mantras* were not correctly uttered as they were remembered to have been uttered at the time of success.

Besides the spirit of the rain in the above example there were the spirits of wind, of this

Various spirits

or that disease, and so on. Various spirits were thought of as fond of various objects for coming down and temporarily resting therein or thereupon and fond also of several animals for food; for instance, the Kol people know the Bongās or spirits by the names of their favourite food: Merom (goat) Bongā, Shim (fowl) Bongā, etc., are the names of some of the spirits. The special sort of stone which the wizards ascertained to be the lovely dwelling of a spirit was brought into the house by many for daily worship. In some cases the hillock itself was held sacred by the worshippers. These are things which are called fetishes by the anthropologists. As in modern times the scientists associate one sort of disease with one microbe and another with another, so various diseases were regarded as associated with this or that spirit.

Fetishes

In the Peninsular India, when there is an outbreak of an epidemic, the medicine-man knows which deity of which particular physical form should be built and worshipped in the village to carry away the disease or diseases.

When the session for worship of the deity is over, the deity is turned away in the following manner. The deity is raised up on the shoulders of the worshippers and slowly carried away from the village, keeping the face of the deity fixed towards the village while the beating of drums and dancing go on in front. The deity in being carried away is expected to think that the worshippers are worshipping it in the village while carrying away all diseases. The worshippers coming at the boundary of the village throw the deity suddenly into a pit or into dead water to bury the diseases there. It is perhaps well known that carrying away of the deity in similar fashion is in vogue in Bengal, though in the worship of the deity no deception is tried to be imposed upon it.

Absence of moral ideas in worship

It is notorious that some robbers and thieves, before going out to execute their object, worship those deities which are believed to grant success to the worshippers, no matter if the object be moral or not. By the force of incantations or *mantras* the deities are believed to be compelled to grant success without caring to maintain the moral order of the world ; the deities simply want to be appeased by the prayers and sacrifices offered by the worshippers.

Inferences drawn from foregoing practices

Both in animism and magical practices we notice first of all the strong desire on the part of man to know the secrets of nature to become happy in life by avoiding or overcoming all sorts of diseases and mishaps the flesh is heir to. This is the very desire which actuates all scientific men to know properly the relations of things in nature, *i.e.*, to know the character of all laws in force in the world. The animists and magicians were misdirected, but one and the same human feeling has been always at work, as may be noticed. The men in their wild savage life performed all their rites to live long, or for the matter of that, to avoid death altogether. The scientists to-day are also trying to discover means by which an indefinitely long life might be secured even though they would fail to possess the means by which death itself might be avoided and the Rubicon finally crossed. From the very first day of human existence till now there has been continuing this prayer in man or in man's life (whether uttered or not): 'From the cradle to the grave, Save, O, save.'

We have hitherto spoken of the ancient popular faith of worshipping and appeasing the ghosts and spirits of nature in which man's relation with his Creator has not been clearly formulated as a definite article of religious faith. A sharp line of demarcation has been proposed to be drawn by some anthropologists between that old faith and the faith in evidence in modern higher culture in which the Creator as the Supreme Being is declared to be the only object of worship. It is not, however, denied by anthropologists that the idea of the Supreme Being presiding over the world was not absent among men of lower culture, though any system of worshipping Him was not brought into use. It has rather been definitely admitted by the scientific investigators of human faiths that there have been some men in all ages who recognised and asserted the existence of One Supreme God, though the need for His worship was not perhaps generally insisted upon. The ideas of the Savara-Kol people in this matter may be examined. It has been the idea with these people that there is a Supreme Being, a Mārāng Bongā (*mārāng*, great, and *bongā*, unseen spirit) who has been the creator of everything. They do not think that this Mārāng Bongā may be inclined to treat men cruelly or to put them to death, having himself created them. They think that as cruel animals make depredations so the malevolent spirits bring miseries to men, and that men can live happily if the malevolent spirits can be appeased. This seems to be, and to have been, the leading idea of all people of lower culture worshipping and appeasing spirits. The writer of these pages has not met with any class of people anywhere in India which does not believe in the existence of One Supreme God, though for practical needs of life spirits only are worshipped to secure good luck or avoid bad.

The idea of Supreme Being

Is demarcation between old and new possible?

To take account of faiths of all shades among the peoples of higher culture is impossible here; the essential elements of one or two religious systems of advanced nations may only be compared with the elements of primitive belief to see if a clear line of demarcation can be drawn between the old and the new. We had occasion to notice previously that in some matters, say in holding the dead body far more sacred than the living body of a man, the proud modern people have retained (maybe unawares) the notions of their savage ancestors. Faith in magic may be considered by some to have died out, but to associate good luck or bad luck with the sight of some objects or with some days or with any particular number is definitely noticeable in all societies, though the declared faith is in the orderly dispensation of God alone. How ill luck is sought to be averted by doing this or that act of no scientific value independently of the prescribed rules occurring in religious codes, is too well known to be mentioned;

notions of old days are hard to die out and to get away from our heritage is exceedinly difficult.

Old notions survive

Not the *natural causes* but their *supernatural seemings* are very much prized by many cultured persons of even scientific training; when expert medical men pronounce some cultured men incurable, these latter in a large number of cases do not resign themselves to their inevitable destiny but run to the 'nearest quack' who holds out hopes of recovery by resorting to methods not dissimilar to the methods of the old-time medicine men. Medicinal drugs pretended to have been discovered in dreams by persons not having the least training in the science of medicine are welcomed in preference to medicines scientifically discovered. Without, therefore, drawing any line of demarcation as referred to above we should in a work like this notice how the sentiments underlying all religious systems have been working and are likely to work. We should notice which way the wind blows.

The Urge of Life and prayer.

We have spoken several times of the urge of life for more, which is a phenomenon of the highest value in life, to notice the unavoidable tendencies or the natural inborn tropisms exhibited in all activities. This urge of life for more may fitly be called the prayers of man, either unconsciously expressed in the activities of life or consciously uttered by man while desiring for progress. Life is, therefore, a bundle of prayers. There is an abiding unshaken hope that the prayers would be answered even though it is the matter of daily experience with man that hope ebbs and flows like the waves.

The prayers may be offered to a ghost, to a spirit of nature, or to God as the Supreme Ruler, or to a blind Fate, but there is an underlying *faith* in this act in the protective character and orderliness of the laws of nature. The conception as to the Ruler or rulers of destiny has been changing ever since, but the prayer of man has been one and the same through all times as a component part of the foundation of religion in this or that form. We are reminded of the pithy expression of poet Carducci: 'Gods depart, but prayers remain.'

Man does not live by bread alone

Innocently to amuse the imagination in this dream of life is wisdom. This line of Goldsmith is quoted to note the inherent ideality of man. We notice that the labourers who work hard all day to earn their daily bread do not care to take their much needed rest for a good while at the end of the day's work but assemble to amuse themselves by singing loud and dancing vigorously. To feel happy they do not mind exhaustion that way and they do really become happy and refreshed by satisfying the cravings of the mind. This is not a small thing to study the tendencies of life.

We notice next how in some matters men have ever since been regardless of economy to satisfy their fancy. The savage people of remote old days who had to work diligently every day to earn a living and could not afford to remain idle any day, as they could not in those days store much food in their houses because of the generally perishable nature of the foodstuff, worked hard to secure such articles as they had fancy for in adorning their person. From great distant places they collected shells, bones, and bright-looking stones solely for personal decoration. Dr. Lowie has remarked that what the savages did for personal decoration involved an 'enormous' cost considering the amount of labour spent upon securing articles of fancy, disregarding the comfortable economic living. How the savage people found great delight in carving wood and in the work of painting to decorate their houses not for a commercial object, has been noticed by many anthropologists. It is true, as Dr. Lowie says, that fashion has its victims on all levels of culture during all times, but how fashion originated and why uneconomically men could be induced to devote time to art must be carefully considered in order to get at the root of the ideality of man.

Real elements in religion

In fine we consider in this connection how human beings have been influenced by the abiding perception of an eternity which has been a special possession of theirs. We do not know and cannot explain the why of it, but it is an undeniable fact that when men allow for a while the eternity to peep into the mind they get solace of an uncommon kind. It may be partly due to relaxation of thoughts but it has to be observed that relaxation of thoughts follows merely as a consequence of eternity streaming into the mind. To direct attention to eternity should not be confused with that questioning attitude of mind which leads men to philosophising. The more the mind is unsophisticated and freed from those thoughts which metaphysical dissertations of the theologicians burden us with, the greater the chance for mind to get that solace. Keats who was never known to have any pronounced theistic inclination lost himself as it were in thoughts of eternity, and could shake off thereby all painful thoughts associated with life; his memorable line addressed to the Nightingale discloses this condition which runs as:

> " Fade far away, dissolve and quite forget,
> What thou amongst the trees hast never known."

The charming Eternity

More or less all men, in proportion no doubt to their culture, taste the sweetness of the eter nity ever abiding in the mind, and neither theistic nor atheistic disposition has anything to do with it. It can never be regarded as unnatural in the least if men attuning themselves to eternity should open their minds, laden with the thoughts of sorrow and miseries, to this eternity. In opening up the gates of their prayers the men may not at all think of getting their wrongs redressed but the very touch of the eternity brings solace to them. This is in a manner to get the prayers heard though nothing may be obtained in response to the items of prayers asking for this or that. This faith inherited from our remotest ancestors still holds the field that prayers to be above want and to get salvation in the end, to be efficacious, must be muttered by following this or that theological prescription ; this ruling faith may one day die down to the very root, but the value of the direct experience of getting much solace and of getting refreshed in life in the presence of the eternal can never suffer any diminution.

If for this solace men look to the eternal void to get aroma of the flower that blossoms in the void, which may be called the *ākāśa-kusum* or unreal imaginary flower, we cannot call them deluded or superstitious. One disposed to theistic thoughts would naturally associate lovely and lovable thoughts of God with the aroma of the imaginary flower.

This special possession of man, of thoughts of eternity, is an abiding factor which underlies all reilgious systems. Men are bound to brood over it, no matter what they might think according to their different creed to be the destiny. It appears rather clear that it is *not the fear* of Nature or of Nature's God that leads to the essential sentiment for religion; what leads is love, enshrined in beauty.

Note.—Westermarck's History of Human Marriage and the author's Jīvana-vānī in Bengali which discusses almost all questions relating to marriage and religion may be consulted.

Explanation of some Terms of Religious Systems.

Animism.—It is to believe in spiritual beings (Tylor). 'The spiritual being is supposed to be an indwelling personality capable of leaving the body or other physical abode and manifesting itself as a phantom.' The Santals like the Mundas and their other congeners believe in such *Bongas*.

Animatism—is the attribution of life and personality to things but not of a separable or apparitional soul.

Naturism—is the worship of Nature. According to Tylor this is part of animism. According to Max Müller this is the beginning of religion. This is found in the Rig Veda.

Fetishism—from West African *fetich* which was a carved human effigy or other object which was prayed to or sacrificed to only when it was supposed to be the temporary abode of some spirit or god, otherwise no regard was paid to it.

Magic.—Trying to create forces of nature or some individual by spells, incantations, etc., as distinguished from religion which recognises a Supreme Being or Superior Beings and offers prayers to them. According to Frazer, magic everywhere preceded religion.

Magical rites are either (1) *sympathetic*—as between a part and a whole when a hair or nail injures the person to whom it belongs or when two things or persons are in contact with each other as a weapon and a man or two friends, or (2) *imitative*—as when like causes like, *e.g.*, inverting a pot imitating the sky and sprinkling water on it, supposed to bring rain; or *e.g.*, wearing eye-like cowry shells, supposed to protect us from the evil eye.

Totemism—Primitive worship of animals or plants or inanimate objects or objects of Nature by clans or groups to whom they are supposed to be related as ancestor as in Australia or India; or to whom they offer protection as guardian-spirits as in America; or against whom or which there is the prohibition against killing or eating as in Africa (Wissler). The Red Indian of North America used to speak of *totam*, his supernatural protector, from which the word totemism is derived. 'A totem is a class of material objects which a savage regards with superstitious respect believing that there exists between him and every member of the class an intimate and altogether special relation' (Frazer). The word is said to be derived from *dodaim* which means village or the residence of a family group.

Pre-animism—or *naturalism*, according to Marrett, is a belief in an impersonal power found amongst many primitive tribes which preceded the stage of animism. Thus, according to Risley, 'All over Chota Nagpur we find sacred groves, the abode of equally indeterminate things who are represented by no symbols and of whose form and function no one can give an intelligible account. They have not yet been clothed with individual attributes; they linger on as survivals of the impersonal state of religion!'

Supreme Being.—Many primitive tribes have belief in a Supreme Being who is considered as being quite apart from other gods. According to Pater Schmidt this belief in a *High-god* is found amongst the primitive tribes with the lowest material culture.

Superior Beings.—Belief in some sort of supernatural beings with superhuman power as gods or angels is found amongst primitive and more advanced peoples.

Personal God or Gods.—When Supreme or superior beings are individualised.

Impersonal Power.—The belief in an impersonal power or energy working at the back of the power of supreme beings is known in many places. Thus amongst the Polynesians this is spoken of as *mānā*, in North America this was spoken of as *Worenda* or *Wakunda*. In the Upanishads there is a beautiful story how Indra could not drench, Agni could not burn, Vayu could not blow away a strip of straw without the aid of all-pervading *Energy* which appeared to them afterwards personified as *Umā Haimavatī*.

APPENDIX

Some Illustrations of the Life of some Primitive Hunters, Fishers, Herdsmen and Agriculturists and Explanation of some Technical Terms

Ethnography deals with the description of the life, manners, customs, religious beliefs, in short, with the material culture and socio-religious institutions of primitive peoples. W. H. R. River's book on the Todas, Hutton's book on the Angami Nagas, S. C. Roy's book on the Birhors, etc., are ethnographic works.

Anthropography is the description of races. This is also called *Ethnology*. Thus when we say that the Bengalis and Gujratis belong, like the peoples of the central belt of Europe or the Irish and the French, probably to the Alpine race, our description belongs to anthropography.

Demography is an extensive and intensive survey of a population or a group of people, by noting evidences of change in constitution, growth or decline of the group or any other ethnic change therein and by specially studying whether the population is sparse or dense, growing, declining, or stationary and by ascertaining the social and biological causes thereof. Thus demography points out that though the primitive peoples of India could thrive well previously, they are now declining or slowly disappearing like some other primitive tribes in the Pacific Islands and at other places.

Primitive peoples could be studied first of all in relation to the place they live in, *i.e.*, their habitat. Human life on earth varies with the climatic conditions and natural resources of the various regions. The vegetation of the zones in which man lives varies according to its nature as to whether it is forest land of the temperate or tropical regions, or as to whether it is cold or hot desert or grass land. In the cold deserts of Tundra which is covered with ice, life is very hard to sustain. Eskimos with their ice-houses and for food and clothing depending on seal-skins with their wheelless sledges may be considered as typical of such a tract. In the equatorial forests where light often does not penetrate even in the daytime we have in Africa or in Brazil some of the most primitive type, often dwarfish in stature and living mostly by hunting. The grass-lands of the steppes of Central Asia generally hold nomadic herdsmen whose wealth consists of cattle, sheep, goat or horses and who have to move about from place to place. It is in the temperate regions of the world that civilization of a high order and stable type has tended to grow. Whether on the banks of the Indus or on the Tigris and Euphratis or on the Nile the fertility of the soil and the more favourable conditions of the climate have made these the centres of early civilization.

Primitive peoples may also be studied according to the stages of their culture. Thus the simplest groups would be hunters who will hunt or trap animals for food and where the women will collect roots and fruits—merely fruit-gatherers. From fruit-gathering possibly developed crude agriculture when from the digging stick the hoe developed. The herdsmen or pastoral people keep domestic animals. Possibly hunting one kind of animal developed the domestication of some animals. Some of the herdsmen of pastoral peoples as in Africa have developed strong warlike communities. The agriculturists are more progressive and with them begins settled life.

Primitive peoples are also studied as belonging to different levels or strata or cycles of culture; thus the pygmy culture is supposed to be the most primitive as illustrated by the Andamanese or the Tasmanians. A little higher type is that of the Australians; then comes the culture of some totemic peoples followed by types in which matriarchy prevailed.. The intermediate types of culture follow next as among Pacific peoples or certain parts of Africa (Sudan) or in the Arctic regions. Then come the pastoral cultures over which have grown civilizations of China, India, Islam, Southern Europe and modern Europe.

ANDAMANESE AS PRIMITIVE FISHING-FOLK

The Andamanese are supposed to be the only people on earth who do not know how to make fire. Their habitation consists of simple wind-screens as protection from the wind. Their dress is very simple—just a waist-belt. They are divided into twelve tribes and they are grouped into three divisions as North Andaman group, South Andaman group and the Little Andaman group. Each tribe is composed of several sub-divisions or septs. Further they are distinguished mainly either as 'Av-yanto' or coast-dwellers and 'Erem-taga' or jungle-dwellers. The former obtain their food chiefly from the sea and are expert at swimming, diving, shooting fish with their bow and arrow while the latter hunt pigs in the jungle with arrows. They live on fish, crabs, etc., in water creeks and flesh of wild pig, wild honey, roots, fruits and seeds from the forest. About ten families generally live in a village. Parties of two to five men go out a-hunting, each man carrying his bow and two or three pig arrows and one carrying a smouldering fire-brand. The women supply the household with vegetable food, fire wood and water. When not hunting the men make bows, arrows, stone adzes, etc. The hunting grounds belong to the whole group and all the members have a right to hunt. The food obtained is equally distributed and affairs are regulated by elderly men and women. They are all strictly monogamous. They believe in spirits of the jungles (*Lau*) or of the sea (*Jurua*) or of the sky (*Morua*) and the dead people also become spirits. The spirits are believed to cause all sickness.

These aborigines of the Andaman islands in the Bay of Bengal belong to the Negrito race and are said to be related to the Semangs of the Malay Peninsula and the Aetas of the Philippines.

The Veddas—a Primitive Hunting Folk

The Veddas live in the eastern part of the island of Ceylon. They are grouped into coast, village and forest people and are classed as Pre-Dravidians. The forest Veddas live solely by hunting. They move their household and camp from season to season near places where game and food is available. In the rains they live in caves or rock shelters which are then partitioned by small blocks of stones into quarters for the different families. Food is cooked by women and shared by all in the rock-shelter. The Vedda is strictly monogamous and the husband generally lives with the wife's family. Descent is traced matrilineally and the father's sister's daughter is preferentially married. The local groups of the Veddas are generally independent and exercise strict control over their own hunting tract of land. No trespassing of land belonging to other groups is tolerated. Objects of personal use are however reckoned as personal property. When a person dies the dead body is left in the cave or rock shelter which is deserted. Their belief is in the spirits of the dead called *yaku* who produce illness, etc. Their rites consist mainly of dances and offerings for the propitiation of the *yaku*, spirits of the dead.

The Toda Herdsmen and Polyandry

The Todas live in the Nilgiri hills very near Ootacamund and are a purely pastoral people. Their whole life centres round their buffaloes and the dairies have become objects of elaborate ritual. They are tall brown people, long-headed, fine- or medium-nosed and highly intelligent. They keep ordinary and sacred buffaloes and there are village dairies and special dairies. They are divided into two divisions and each consists of several clans. Marriage with daughter of the mother's brother or of the father's sister is preferred. These children of brothers and sisters are *matchuni*. When a woman marries a man she becomes the wife of his brothers at the same time. The husbands may be clan brothers if not own brothers. When the child is in the womb, the eldest brother generally performs the bow-and-arrow ceremony and is regarded as the father. The brothers generally have more than one wife and they are equally the wives of all. Thus polygamy is combined with polyandry. Land, village dairies and some sacred buffaloes are owned by the clan, house and some lands are owned by the family, while buffaloes, household goods, etc., are the property of the individual. Each clan has generally a headman chosen for his character and ability. The women are excluded from religious ceremonials connected with the dairy and have distinctly an inferior status. The Todas with fraternal polyandry are definitely patrilineal.

Matrilineal Nayars

The Nayars who are sung of in the great Portuguese epic as 'By the proud Nayars the noble rank is claimed' and who have been described as 'having no other profession but that of arms' who 'eating rice from the hands of the king promised to burn themselves if the king died or was slain and punctually fulfilled their promise' are the great gentry of the Malabar coast. They are important as being examples of non-fraternal polyandry as practised amongst them once though now extinct (as the Todas are examples of fraternal polyandry). Hamilton and Buchanan described that amongst them 'a woman had several husbands but these were not brothers.' 'When a man goes into his wife's house and leaves his arms at the door, none dare remove them or enter the house at pain of death. The husbands agree very well for they consort with her in their turns. The children are never heir to their father's estate, but the father's sister's children are' (Hamilton, 1727). Thus 'all inheritances among the Nayars go to their brothers or sons of their sisters, born of the same mothers, all relationship being counted on female consanguinity and descent' (Russell).

Matrilineal Khasi and Garo and their Junogeniture

The Khasis are the well-known people of the Khasi Hills round Shillong, while the Garos inhabit the Garo Hills at the western end of the range of hills which form the southern boundary of the Brahmaputra valley. They are both noteworthy as having descent in the female line and in both it is the youngest daughter who inherits the property (junogeniture) as in English law the eldest son inherits (primogeniture), just as Jacob got the property of the father instead of the elder brother Esau in the Bible. But the other Assam tribes are generally patrilineal while these two and just a few others more or less allied to them are matrilineal.

Amongst the Khasis there are many clans which trace their descent from ancestresses or *Kiaw* (grandmothers). The family generally consists of the grandmother, her daughters and her daughters' children living under the same roof, the grandmother being the head of the house. The state is well organised under a chief or *Siem* in each of the several Khasi estates. Succession to this office of siemship through the female side goes to the sons of the eldest uterine sister in contrast to inheritance which always goes to the youngest daughter. Succession to the office of a priestess is also often by the eldest surviving daughter. The mother's brother (*kui*) is the head of the house but the father is the executive head of the new home as after children have been born, his wife and children live with him. The youngest daughter 'holds the religion' as they say and in her house the family ceremonies are performed. The youngest daughter or youngest female descendant of youngest female heir, is the heir to all property.

Amongst the Garos there are many clans which are called *machongs* or motherhoods. Descent and inheritance are in the female line but the property is always managed by a *nokrom* (from *nok* house, *krung* host). He is generally the youngest son-in-law, and is the son of the former *nokrom's* sister, who has to marry his maternal uncle's daughter. He has to live with his wife's people and is responsible for his adoptive family.

The Khasi language belongs to the Mon-Khmer branch of the Austronesian division of the Austric family of which another branch is the Munda family. Thus linguistically they have affinitics with Mundari-speaking tribes of Chhota Nagpur but racially they are like other Mengoloid tribes of Assam. The Garos speak a Tibeto-Burman language and are racially Mongoloid.